Mometrix

TEST PREPARATION

I0868210

Common Core Grade 9 English Language Arts Secrets Study Guide

DEAR FUTURE EXAM SUCCESS STORY

First of all, **THANK YOU** for purchasing Mometrix study materials!

Second, congratulations! You are one of the few determined test-takers who are committed to doing whatever it takes to excel on your exam. **You have come to the right place.** We developed these study materials with one goal in mind: to deliver you the information you need in a format that's concise and easy to use.

In addition to optimizing your guide for the content of the test, we've outlined our recommended steps for breaking down the preparation process into small, attainable goals so you can make sure you stay on track.

We've also analyzed the entire test-taking process, identifying the most common pitfalls and showing how you can overcome them and be ready for any curveball the test throws you.

Standardized testing is one of the biggest obstacles on your road to success, which only increases the importance of doing well in the high-pressure, high-stakes environment of test day. Your results on this test could have a significant impact on your future, and this guide provides the information and practical advice to help you achieve your full potential on test day.

Your success is our success

We would love to hear from you! If you would like to share the story of your exam success or if you have any questions or comments in regard to our products, please contact us at **800-673-8175** or **support@mometrix.com**.

Thanks again for your business and we wish you continued success!

Sincerely,
The Mometrix Test Preparation Team

Need more help? Check out our flashcards at:
http://MometrixFlashcards.com/CCSS

Written and edited by the Mometrix Exam Secrets Test Prep Team
Printed in the United States of America

TABLE OF CONTENTS

Introduction

Thank you for purchasing this resource! You have made the choice to prepare yourself for a test that could have a huge impact on your future, and this guide is designed to help you be fully ready for test day. Obviously, it's important to have a solid understanding of the test material, but you also need to be prepared for the unique environment and stressors of the test, so that you can perform to the best of your abilities.

For this purpose, the first section that appears in this guide is the **Secret Keys**. We've devoted countless hours to meticulously researching what works and what doesn't, and we've boiled down our findings to the five most impactful steps you can take to improve your performance on the test. We start at the beginning with study planning and move through the preparation process, all the way to the testing strategies that will help you get the most out of what you know when you're finally sitting in front of the test.

We recommend that you start preparing for your test as far in advance as possible. However, if you've bought this guide as a last-minute study resource and only have a few days before your test, we recommend that you skip over the first two Secret Keys since they address a long-term study plan.

If you struggle with **test anxiety**, we strongly encourage you to check out our recommendations for how you can overcome it. Test anxiety is a formidable foe, but it can be beaten, and we want to make sure you have the tools you need to defeat it.

Secret Key #1 – Plan Big, Study Small

There's a lot riding on your performance. If you want to ace this test, you're going to need to keep your skills sharp and the material fresh in your mind. You need a plan that lets you review everything you need to know while still fitting in your schedule. We'll break this strategy down into three categories.

Information Organization

Start with the information you already have: the official test outline. From this, you can make a complete list of all the concepts you need to cover before the test. Organize these concepts into groups that can be studied together, and create a list of any related vocabulary you need to learn so you can brush up on any difficult terms. You'll want to keep this vocabulary list handy once you actually start studying since you may need to add to it along the way.

Time Management

Once you have your set of study concepts, decide how to spread them out over the time you have left before the test. Break your study plan into small, clear goals so you have a manageable task for each day and know exactly what you're doing. Then just focus on one small step at a time. When you manage your time this way, you don't need to spend hours at a time studying. Studying a small block of content for a short period each day helps you retain information better and avoid stressing over how much you have left to do. You can relax knowing that you have a plan to cover everything in time. In order for this strategy to be effective though, you have to start studying early and stick to your schedule. Avoid the exhaustion and futility that comes from last-minute cramming!

Study Environment

The environment you study in has a big impact on your learning. Studying in a coffee shop, while probably more enjoyable, is not likely to be as fruitful as studying in a quiet room. It's important to keep distractions to a minimum. You're only planning to study for a short block of time, so make the most of it. Don't pause to check your phone or get up to find a snack. It's also important to **avoid multitasking**. Research has consistently shown that multitasking will make your studying dramatically less effective. Your study area should also be comfortable and well-lit so you don't have the distraction of straining your eyes or sitting on an uncomfortable chair.

The time of day you study is also important. You want to be rested and alert. Don't wait until just before bedtime. Study when you'll be most likely to comprehend and remember. Even better, if you know what time of day your test will be, set that time aside for study. That way your brain will be used to working on that subject at that specific time and you'll have a better chance of recalling information.

Finally, it can be helpful to team up with others who are studying for the same test. Your actual studying should be done in as isolated an environment as possible, but the work of organizing the information and setting up the study plan can be divided up. In between study sessions, you can discuss with your teammates the concepts that you're all studying and quiz each other on the details. Just be sure that your teammates are as serious about the test as you are. If you find that your study time is being replaced with social time, you might need to find a new team.

Secret Key #2 – Make Your Studying Count

You're devoting a lot of time and effort to preparing for this test, so you want to be absolutely certain it will pay off. This means doing more than just reading the content and hoping you can remember it on test day. It's important to make every minute of study count. There are two main areas you can focus on to make your studying count.

Retention

It doesn't matter how much time you study if you can't remember the material. You need to make sure you are retaining the concepts. To check your retention of the information you're learning, try recalling it at later times with minimal prompting. Try carrying around flashcards and glance at one or two from time to time or ask a friend who's also studying for the test to quiz you.

To enhance your retention, look for ways to put the information into practice so that you can apply it rather than simply recalling it. If you're using the information in practical ways, it will be much easier to remember. Similarly, it helps to solidify a concept in your mind if you're not only reading it to yourself but also explaining it to someone else. Ask a friend to let you teach them about a concept you're a little shaky on (or speak aloud to an imaginary audience if necessary). As you try to summarize, define, give examples, and answer your friend's questions, you'll understand the concepts better and they will stay with you longer. Finally, step back for a big picture view and ask yourself how each piece of information fits with the whole subject. When you link the different concepts together and see them working together as a whole, it's easier to remember the individual components.

Finally, practice showing your work on any multi-step problems, even if you're just studying. Writing out each step you take to solve a problem will help solidify the process in your mind, and you'll be more likely to remember it during the test.

Modality

Modality simply refers to the means or method by which you study. Choosing a study modality that fits your own individual learning style is crucial. No two people learn best in exactly the same way, so it's important to know your strengths and use them to your advantage.

For example, if you learn best by visualization, focus on visualizing a concept in your mind and draw an image or a diagram. Try color-coding your notes, illustrating them, or creating symbols that will trigger your mind to recall a learned concept. If you learn best by hearing or discussing information, find a study partner who learns the same way or read aloud to yourself. Think about how to put the information in your own words. Imagine that you are giving a lecture on the topic and record yourself so you can listen to it later.

For any learning style, flashcards can be helpful. Organize the information so you can take advantage of spare moments to review. Underline key words or phrases. Use different colors for different categories. Mnemonic devices (such as creating a short list in which every item starts with the same letter) can also help with retention. Find what works best for you and use it to store the information in your mind most effectively and easily.

Secret Key #3 – Practice the Right Way

Your success on test day depends not only on how many hours you put into preparing, but also on whether you prepared the right way. It's good to check along the way to see if your studying is paying off. One of the most effective ways to do this is by taking practice tests to evaluate your progress. Practice tests are useful because they show exactly where you need to improve. Every time you take a practice test, pay special attention to these three groups of questions:

- The questions you got wrong
- The questions you had to guess on, even if you guessed right
- The questions you found difficult or slow to work through

This will show you exactly what your weak areas are, and where you need to devote more study time. Ask yourself why each of these questions gave you trouble. Was it because you didn't understand the material? Was it because you didn't remember the vocabulary? Do you need more repetitions on this type of question to build speed and confidence? Dig into those questions and figure out how you can strengthen your weak areas as you go back to review the material.

Additionally, many practice tests have a section explaining the answer choices. It can be tempting to read the explanation and think that you now have a good understanding of the concept. However, an explanation likely only covers part of the question's broader context. Even if the explanation makes perfect sense, **go back and investigate** every concept related to the question until you're positive you have a thorough understanding.

As you go along, keep in mind that the practice test is just that: practice. Memorizing these questions and answers will not be very helpful on the actual test because it is unlikely to have any of the same exact questions. If you only know the right answers to the sample questions, you won't be prepared for the real thing. **Study the concepts** until you understand them fully, and then you'll be able to answer any question that shows up on the test.

It's important to wait on the practice tests until you're ready. If you take a test on your first day of study, you may be overwhelmed by the amount of material covered and how much you need to learn. Work up to it gradually.

On test day, you'll need to be prepared for answering questions, managing your time, and using the test-taking strategies you've learned. It's a lot to balance, like a mental marathon that will have a big impact on your future. Like training for a marathon, you'll need to start slowly and work your way up. When test day arrives, you'll be ready.

Start with the strategies you've read in the first two Secret Keys—plan your course and study in the way that works best for you. If you have time, consider using multiple study resources to get different approaches to the same concepts. It can be helpful to see difficult concepts from more than one angle. Then find a good source for practice tests. Many times, the test website will suggest potential study resources or provide sample tests.

Practice Test Strategy

If you're able to find at least three practice tests, we recommend this strategy:

Untimed and Open-Book Practice

Take the first test with no time constraints and with your notes and study guide handy. Take your time and focus on applying the strategies you've learned.

Timed and Open-Book Practice

Take the second practice test open-book as well, but set a timer and practice pacing yourself to finish in time.

Timed and Closed-Book Practice

Take any other practice tests as if it were test day. Set a timer and put away your study materials. Sit at a table or desk in a quiet room, imagine yourself at the testing center, and answer questions as quickly and accurately as possible.

Keep repeating timed and closed-book tests on a regular basis until you run out of practice tests or it's time for the actual test. Your mind will be ready for the schedule and stress of test day, and you'll be able to focus on recalling the material you've learned.

Secret Key #4 – Pace Yourself

Once you're fully prepared for the material on the test, your biggest challenge on test day will be managing your time. Just knowing that the clock is ticking can make you panic even if you have plenty of time left. Work on pacing yourself so you can build confidence against the time constraints of the exam. Pacing is a difficult skill to master, especially in a high-pressure environment, so **practice is vital**.

Set time expectations for your pace based on how much time is available. For example, if a section has 60 questions and the time limit is 30 minutes, you know you have to average 30 seconds or less per question in order to answer them all. Although 30 seconds is the hard limit, set 25 seconds per question as your goal, so you reserve extra time to spend on harder questions. When you budget extra time for the harder questions, you no longer have any reason to stress when those questions take longer to answer.

Don't let this time expectation distract you from working through the test at a calm, steady pace, but keep it in mind so you don't spend too much time on any one question. Recognize that taking extra time on one question you don't understand may keep you from answering two that you do understand later in the test. If your time limit for a question is up and you're still not sure of the answer, mark it and move on, and come back to it later if the time and the test format allow. If the testing format doesn't allow you to return to earlier questions, just make an educated guess; then put it out of your mind and move on.

On the easier questions, be careful not to rush. It may seem wise to hurry through them so you have more time for the challenging ones, but it's not worth missing one if you know the concept and just didn't take the time to read the question fully. Work efficiently but make sure you understand the question and have looked at all of the answer choices, since more than one may seem right at first.

Even if you're paying attention to the time, you may find yourself a little behind at some point. You should speed up to get back on track, but do so wisely. Don't panic; just take a few seconds less on each question until you're caught up. Don't guess without thinking, but do look through the answer choices and eliminate any you know are wrong. If you can get down to two choices, it is often worthwhile to guess from those. Once you've chosen an answer, move on and don't dwell on any that you skipped or had to hurry through. If a question was taking too long, chances are it was one of the harder ones, so you weren't as likely to get it right anyway.

On the other hand, if you find yourself getting ahead of schedule, it may be beneficial to slow down a little. The more quickly you work, the more likely you are to make a careless mistake that will affect your score. You've budgeted time for each question, so don't be afraid to spend that time. Practice an efficient but careful pace to get the most out of the time you have.

Secret Key #5 – Have a Plan for Guessing

When you're taking the test, you may find yourself stuck on a question. Some of the answer choices seem better than others, but you don't see the one answer choice that is obviously correct. What do you do?

The scenario described above is very common, yet most test takers have not effectively prepared for it. Developing and practicing a plan for guessing may be one of the single most effective uses of your time as you get ready for the exam.

In developing your plan for guessing, there are three questions to address:

- When should you start the guessing process?
- How should you narrow down the choices?
- Which answer should you choose?

When to Start the Guessing Process

Unless your plan for guessing is to select C every time (which, despite its merits, is not what we recommend), you need to leave yourself enough time to apply your answer elimination strategies. Since you have a limited amount of time for each question, that means that if you're going to give yourself the best shot at guessing correctly, you have to decide quickly whether or not you will guess.

Of course, the best-case scenario is that you don't have to guess at all, so first, see if you can answer the question based on your knowledge of the subject and basic reasoning skills. Focus on the key words in the question and try to jog your memory of related topics. Give yourself a chance to bring the knowledge to mind, but once you realize that you don't have (or you can't access) the knowledge you need to answer the question, it's time to start the guessing process.

It's almost always better to start the guessing process too early than too late. It only takes a few seconds to remember something and answer the question from knowledge. Carefully eliminating wrong answer choices takes longer. Plus, going through the process of eliminating answer choices can actually help jog your memory.

Summary: Start the guessing process as soon as you decide that you can't answer the question based on your knowledge.

How to Narrow Down the Choices

The next chapter in this book (**Test-Taking Strategies**) includes a wide range of strategies for how to approach questions and how to look for answer choices to eliminate. You will definitely want to read those carefully, practice them, and figure out which ones work best for you. Here though, we're going to address a mindset rather than a particular strategy.

Your odds of guessing an answer correctly depend on how many options you are choosing from.

Number of options left	5	4	3	2	1
Odds of guessing correctly	20%	25%	33%	50%	100%

You can see from this chart just how valuable it is to be able to eliminate incorrect answers and make an educated guess, but there are two things that many test takers do that cause them to miss out on the benefits of guessing:

- Accidentally eliminating the correct answer
- Selecting an answer based on an impression

We'll look at the first one here, and the second one in the next section.

To avoid accidentally eliminating the correct answer, we recommend a thought exercise called **the $5 challenge**. In this challenge, you only eliminate an answer choice from contention if you are willing to bet $5 on it being wrong. Why $5? Five dollars is a small but not insignificant amount of money. It's an amount you could afford to lose but wouldn't want to throw away. And while losing $5 once might not hurt too much, doing it twenty times will set you back $100. In the same way, each small decision you make—eliminating a choice here, guessing on a question there—won't by itself impact your score very much, but when you put them all together, they can make a big difference. By holding each answer choice elimination decision to a higher standard, you can reduce the risk of accidentally eliminating the correct answer.

The $5 challenge can also be applied in a positive sense: If you are willing to bet $5 that an answer choice *is* correct, go ahead and mark it as correct.

Summary: Only eliminate an answer choice if you are willing to bet $5 that it is wrong.

Which Answer to Choose

You're taking the test. You've run into a hard question and decided you'll have to guess. You've eliminated all the answer choices you're willing to bet $5 on. Now you have to pick an answer. Why do we even need to talk about this? Why can't you just pick whichever one you feel like when the time comes?

The answer to these questions is that if you don't come into the test with a plan, you'll rely on your impression to select an answer choice, and if you do that, you risk falling into a trap. The test writers know that everyone who takes their test will be guessing on some of the questions, so they intentionally write wrong answer choices to seem plausible. You still have to pick an answer though, and if the wrong answer choices are designed to look right, how can you ever be sure that you're not falling for their trap? The best solution we've found to this dilemma is to take the decision out of your hands entirely. Here is the process we recommend:

Once you've eliminated any choices that you are confident (willing to bet $5) are wrong, select the first remaining choice as your answer.

Whether you choose to select the first remaining choice, the second, or the last, the important thing is that you use some preselected standard. Using this approach guarantees that you will not be enticed into selecting an answer choice that looks right, because you are not basing your decision on how the answer choices look.

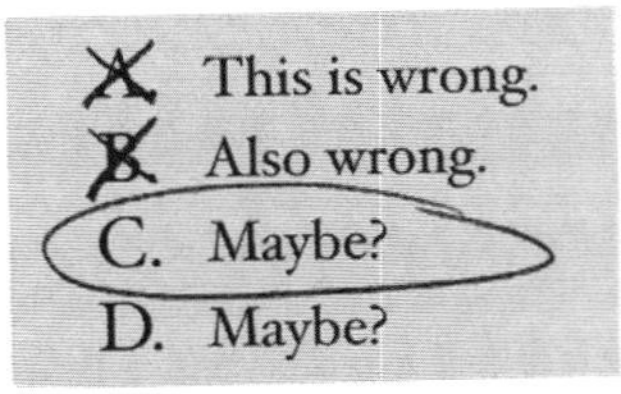

This is not meant to make you question your knowledge. Instead, it is to help you recognize the difference between your knowledge and your impressions. There's a huge difference between thinking an answer is right because of what you know, and thinking an answer is right because it looks or sounds like it should be right.

Summary: To ensure that your selection is appropriately random, make a predetermined selection from among all answer choices you have not eliminated.

Test-Taking Strategies

This section contains a list of test-taking strategies that you may find helpful as you work through the test. By taking what you know and applying logical thought, you can maximize your chances of answering any question correctly!

It is very important to realize that every question is different and every person is different: no single strategy will work on every question, and no single strategy will work for every person. That's why we've included all of them here, so you can try them out and determine which ones work best for different types of questions and which ones work best for you.

Question Strategies

⊘ Read Carefully

Read the question and the answer choices carefully. Don't miss the question because you misread the terms. You have plenty of time to read each question thoroughly and make sure you understand what is being asked. Yet a happy medium must be attained, so don't waste too much time. You must read carefully and efficiently.

⊘ Contextual Clues

Look for contextual clues. If the question includes a word you are not familiar with, look at the immediate context for some indication of what the word might mean. Contextual clues can often give you all the information you need to decipher the meaning of an unfamiliar word. Even if you can't determine the meaning, you may be able to narrow down the possibilities enough to make a solid guess at the answer to the question.

⊘ Prefixes

If you're having trouble with a word in the question or answer choices, try dissecting it. Take advantage of every clue that the word might include. Prefixes can be a huge help. Usually, they allow you to determine a basic meaning. *Pre-* means before, *post-* means after, *pro-* is positive, *de-* is negative. From prefixes, you can get an idea of the general meaning of the word and try to put it into context.

⊘ Hedge Words

Watch out for critical hedge words, such as *likely, may, can, often, almost, mostly, usually, generally, rarely,* and *sometimes.* Question writers insert these hedge phrases to cover every possibility. Often an answer choice will be wrong simply because it leaves no room for exception. Be on guard for answer choices that have definitive words such as *exactly* and *always.*

⊘ Switchback Words

Stay alert for *switchbacks.* These are the words and phrases frequently used to alert you to shifts in thought. The most common switchback words are *but, although,* and *however.* Others include *nevertheless, on the other hand, even though, while, in spite of, despite,* and *regardless of.* Switchback words are important to catch because they can change the direction of the question or an answer choice.

⊘ FACE VALUE

When in doubt, use common sense. Accept the situation in the problem at face value. Don't read too much into it. These problems will not require you to make wild assumptions. If you have to go beyond creativity and warp time or space in order to have an answer choice fit the question, then you should move on and consider the other answer choices. These are normal problems rooted in reality. The applicable relationship or explanation may not be readily apparent, but it is there for you to figure out. Use your common sense to interpret anything that isn't clear.

Answer Choice Strategies

⊘ ANSWER SELECTION

The most thorough way to pick an answer choice is to identify and eliminate wrong answers until only one is left, then confirm it is the correct answer. Sometimes an answer choice may immediately seem right, but be careful. The test writers will usually put more than one reasonable answer choice on each question, so take a second to read all of them and make sure that the other choices are not equally obvious. As long as you have time left, it is better to read every answer choice than to pick the first one that looks right without checking the others.

⊘ ANSWER CHOICE FAMILIES

An answer choice family consists of two (in rare cases, three) answer choices that are very similar in construction and cannot all be true at the same time. If you see two answer choices that are direct opposites or parallels, one of them is usually the correct answer. For instance, if one answer choice says that quantity *x* increases and another either says that quantity *x* decreases (opposite) or says that quantity *y* increases (parallel), then those answer choices would fall into the same family. An answer choice that doesn't match the construction of the answer choice family is more likely to be incorrect. Most questions will not have answer choice families, but when they do appear, you should be prepared to recognize them.

⊘ ELIMINATE ANSWERS

Eliminate answer choices as soon as you realize they are wrong, but make sure you consider all possibilities. If you are eliminating answer choices and realize that the last one you are left with is also wrong, don't panic. Start over and consider each choice again. There may be something you missed the first time that you will realize on the second pass.

⊘ AVOID FACT TRAPS

Don't be distracted by an answer choice that is factually true but doesn't answer the question. You are looking for the choice that answers the question. Stay focused on what the question is asking for so you don't accidentally pick an answer that is true but incorrect. Always go back to the question and make sure the answer choice you've selected actually answers the question and is not merely a true statement.

⊘ EXTREME STATEMENTS

In general, you should avoid answers that put forth extreme actions as standard practice or proclaim controversial ideas as established fact. An answer choice that states the "process should be used in certain situations, if..." is much more likely to be correct than one that states the "process should be discontinued completely." The first is a calm rational statement and doesn't even make a definitive, uncompromising stance, using a hedge word *if* to provide wiggle room, whereas the second choice is far more extreme.

⊘ BENCHMARK

As you read through the answer choices and you come across one that seems to answer the question well, mentally select that answer choice. This is not your final answer, but it's the one that will help you evaluate the other answer choices. The one that you selected is your benchmark or standard for judging each of the other answer choices. Every other answer choice must be compared to your benchmark. That choice is correct until proven otherwise by another answer choice beating it. If you find a better answer, then that one becomes your new benchmark. Once you've decided that no other choice answers the question as well as your benchmark, you have your final answer.

⊘ PREDICT THE ANSWER

Before you even start looking at the answer choices, it is often best to try to predict the answer. When you come up with the answer on your own, it is easier to avoid distractions and traps because you will know exactly what to look for. The right answer choice is unlikely to be word-for-word what you came up with, but it should be a close match. Even if you are confident that you have the right answer, you should still take the time to read each option before moving on.

General Strategies

⊘ TOUGH QUESTIONS

If you are stumped on a problem or it appears too hard or too difficult, don't waste time. Move on! Remember though, if you can quickly check for obviously incorrect answer choices, your chances of guessing correctly are greatly improved. Before you completely give up, at least try to knock out a couple of possible answers. Eliminate what you can and then guess at the remaining answer choices before moving on.

⊘ CHECK YOUR WORK

Since you will probably not know every term listed and the answer to every question, it is important that you get credit for the ones that you do know. Don't miss any questions through careless mistakes. If at all possible, try to take a second to look back over your answer selection and make sure you've selected the correct answer choice and haven't made a costly careless mistake (such as marking an answer choice that you didn't mean to mark). This quick double check should more than pay for itself in caught mistakes for the time it costs.

⊘ PACE YOURSELF

It's easy to be overwhelmed when you're looking at a page full of questions; your mind is confused and full of random thoughts, and the clock is ticking down faster than you would like. Calm down and maintain the pace that you have set for yourself. Especially as you get down to the last few minutes of the test, don't let the small numbers on the clock make you panic. As long as you are on track by monitoring your pace, you are guaranteed to have time for each question.

⊘ DON'T RUSH

It is very easy to make errors when you are in a hurry. Maintaining a fast pace in answering questions is pointless if it makes you miss questions that you would have gotten right otherwise. Test writers like to include distracting information and wrong answers that seem right. Taking a little extra time to avoid careless mistakes can make all the difference in your test score. Find a pace that allows you to be confident in the answers that you select.

⊘ KEEP MOVING

Panicking will not help you pass the test, so do your best to stay calm and keep moving. Taking deep breaths and going through the answer elimination steps you practiced can help to break through a stress barrier and keep your pace.

Final Notes

The combination of a solid foundation of content knowledge and the confidence that comes from practicing your plan for applying that knowledge is the key to maximizing your performance on test day. As your foundation of content knowledge is built up and strengthened, you'll find that the strategies included in this chapter become more and more effective in helping you quickly sift through the distractions and traps of the test to isolate the correct answer.

Now that you're preparing to move forward into the test content chapters of this book, be sure to keep your goal in mind. As you read, think about how you will be able to apply this information on the test. If you've already seen sample questions for the test and you have an idea of the question format and style, try to come up with questions of your own that you can answer based on what you're reading. This will give you valuable practice applying your knowledge in the same ways you can expect to on test day.

Good luck and good studying!

Reading

Literature

Explicit Information

Explicit information is the information stated in a passage or story. It includes facts and statements about the characters in a story as well as about the setting and the events that take place in the story. Explicit information is not merely hinted at; instead, this kind of information is definite, which does not require the reader to draw a conclusion. Explicit information may be found in many forms. It can be in a description, such as "Nora had blue eyes," or in the dialogue "I am from New York City." It also can be found in the actions that characters take. Often this kind of information can be used to support an inference.

Read the following excerpt and identify the explicit information.

> Listen and you will hear the tale of Odin. Odin lived many years ago. He was the head of the gods in what is now Norway. These gods lived in a place called Midgard, and they had many adventures.

Explicit information is information found right within the text, itself. Since explicit information is stated directly in the text, it is not inferred or suggested in any way. The excerpt tells about a god named Odin, who was the head of the gods. They lived in what is now Norway, in a place called Midgard. This information is all explicit, since the passage states it directly. The reader does not need to infer or guess at anything, and nothing is hinted or suggested. Everything is factual, and the reader need not draw a conclusion from the information. When you read, think about the information in the story and whether the information is explicit or not explicit.

Inference

An inference is a conclusion a reader can make from the explicit information found in a passage or story. In addition, an inference often is based on personal experience combined with the information in a passage. For instance, a story may say that a character hears a siren and sees smoke in the distance. From the explicit information in the story and from his or her personal knowledge, the reader can make the logical conclusion that a fire truck is going to a fire. A good inference is supported by the information in a passage. Inferences are not like explicit information, which the passage clearly states. Inferences are not stated in a passage. Instead, the passage hints at inferences. A good reader must put the information together to produce a logical conclusion that is most likely true.

Read the following excerpt and decide why Bonnie liked sailing.

> Bonnie's job was very stressful. She was responsible for looking after several big accounts, and often her phone never stopped ringing. At home at night she would wake up and worry. Watching TV didn't help. But when she was in a boat, with the wind in her face, she forgot all about her job. She could relax.

From this passage, the reader can conclude that Bonnie liked sailing because being in a boat made her feel better. She could relax. The excerpt does not say explicitly that Bonnie liked sailing for these reasons. The reader, however, can infer these reasons for why Bonnie likes sailing. Since sailing made Bonnie relax, it is a "best guess" that Bonnie likes sailing. This is a logical conclusion to the information in the passage, and it is the best conclusion based on what a reader might know from personal experience. An inference is based on the information in a passage and a reader's experience, but it is not stated in the text.

Discovering the Theme of a Story

The theme of a story is the lesson that it teaches, or the moral or what the reader learns from the story. Some themes are used and reused. These themes are called universal themes, and they are related to life, society, human nature, and common situations that arise. Some universal themes include man vs. man or man vs. nature. Other similar themes are "Goodness is rewarded," or "Life evens out." Themes are an important aspect of literature since it teaches the reader or listener a truth about life. The theme is developed by the story's plot and how a character or characters respond to situations in the story.

Tell why the theme of the excerpt should be "Overconfidence brings a fall."

> One day Conrad bet his friend Billy that he could beat him running, so they had a contest. Billy knew he wasn't very fast, but he kept going. Conrad, who was very fast, started off quickly, but then he stopped to talk to people. Billy passed Conrad by the side of the road and won.

The excerpt tells the story of a boy who bet he could beat his friend in a race. Conrad was faster than Billy, but Billy ended up winning the race. Billy kept going, while Conrad was so confident of the win that he stopped to talk to some people. The story's main point teaches a lesson. If you are overly confident you may have a fall. The theme of a story is the lesson it teaches, and in this excerpt the slower runner who keeps going wins over the faster runner. This universal theme is found often in literature. The fable of the Rabbit and Turtle has a similar theme, but a fable states the theme or moral at the end of the story. Other kinds of fiction do not state the theme at the end of the story.

Components of a Summary

A summary of a story has several components. It should include the main ideas of the passage and also the most important details. These details should support the main idea. A summary is not just a general statement about the story, nor is a summary a paraphrase. Paraphrases reword the main idea and give many supporting ideas in greater detail; summaries do not. A summary will not include everything in the story. In order to write an objective summary, you will need to think about what happens in the story. You will need to decide what is the story is mostly about and what details are most important to the main idea. Summaries are useful since they allow a reader to remember the main idea and the most important details.

Development of Characters

Characters are central to a story. Characters' conflicts and problems make a story interesting and complex. With each event of a story, a character reveals himself or herself to the reader. How characters deal with conflict tells a great deal about their character. How they deal with other characters also tells about what they are feeling. Characters and their actions advance the plot because they show the way in which a story is developing. The way in which characters react tells the reader a great deal about their nature. They also help the reader understand the theme or lesson that the story teaches. Characters' ultimate outcome is central to the development of the theme of a story.

Explain how the two characters interact with each other.

> Veronica felt her knees shaking as the gym class began. She looked at the rope stretching up to the ceiling. She took the rope in one hand. She kept thinking what would happen if she fell. Then

> she heard her friend Alice call out, "You can do it, kiddo!" She smiled. Hand over hand; she started to climb up the rope.

In the passage, Veronica feels the conflict of fear or failure. She is worried about climbing the rope. She wonders what will happen if she falls while climbing the rope. The reader does not know why Veronica is afraid, but her shaking knees tell the reader of the tension Veronica is feeling. The setting is the school gym. After her friend Alice calls out words of encouragement, Veronica's demeanor changes and she smiles. Her fear of failure is gone, and she begins to climb the rope. The two characters obviously are close friends, and Alice's words change Veronica and give her strength to challenge the rope. This is how they interact with one another.

Explain how the character in the excerpt shapes the theme.

> Norman put his hands on the wheel. He looked at the driving officer who nodded to begin. Norman pulled out. He followed the officer's instructions. Norman wondered if his nervousness showed. He thought about all the lessons he had taken, and how they all led to this point. It seemed like an eternity before he heard the words, "You passed."

The setting is the inside of a car, and the plot revolves around Norman as he begins to take the road test for his driver's license, one of the biggest events in any teenager's life. The conflict revolves around whether he will pass or fail. Norman remembers his Driver's Ed lessons, and the many hours he spent in a car with his teacher. The theme is definitely coming of age. Norman shapes the theme by being lost in concentration and trying not to make a mistake until he hears the words he had hoped for: "You passed." The theme is intertwined with Norman's emotions. He shapes the theme.

Context Clues

The best way to figure out the meaning of unknown words and expressions is to examine the surrounding context clues. Often many clues to the meaning of an expression or word in the sentences occur just before or after the unknown word or expression. Some words have more than one meaning, and only through the context of the text can these words be understood. For instance, the word "blunt" has several meanings, including "having a dull edge," "not being subtle," and "being slow to understand," so understanding the context is important. In the sentence, "He was a blunt talker, and I got his point quickly," it becomes clear that the meaning is "not being subtle." Phrases also must be understood through context. In the sentence, "She rolled up her sleeves and got to work," the reader can get the sense that "rolling up her sleeves" means to get ready for hard work.

Figurative Language

Figurative language is the use of words and expressions to expand reality in a vivid way. An author can use language in a non-literal way, which means using language in a non-traditional manner in order to create an image. Examples of figurative language include simile, metaphor, personification, and hyperbole as well as onomatopoeia and alliteration. Similes compare things using the words *like* or *as,* for example, "He is strong as an ox." Metaphors compare things without using comparing words, for example, "He is an ox when it comes to work." Personification gives a thing or animal human traits, for example, "The trees talked to me of days gone by." Hyperbole is an exaggeration that is not believable: "He is the most exciting individual that exists on the planet."Onomatopoeia is when words sound like what they are, "moo, moo"; and alliteration involves using words successively that start with the same letter: "Baa, baa, black sheep...."

READ THE EXCERPT.

Jim watched with awe as Marianne sliced her way effortlessly through the commuters crowded together in the train station.

TELL WHAT FORM THE PHRASE "SLICED ITS WAY EFFORTLESSLY" IS AND WHY.

The phrase "sliced her way effortlessly" is an example of a figure of speech called a metaphor. Metaphors add depth to writing and make it richer. They are used to create a more vivid image of something in the reader's mind, in this case like a knife easily slicing through something without any resistance, like a piece of cake. This example is not a simile because it doesn't use a word such as "like" to compare two things. It can't be hyperbole, since the phrase is not an exaggeration. This phrase is not an example of personification because Marianne is human.

DENOTATIVE AND CONNOTATIVE MEANINGS OF WORDS

A word can have both a denotative meaning and a connotative meaning. The denotative meaning is the actual meaning of a word. The connotative meaning refers to the associations a word has above and beyond its literal meaning. For instance, the word "frugal" might mean "careful with money" or "economical," while the word "miserly" adds another dimension to the understanding of what someone is like. "Miserly" has a much more negative connotation than does "frugal." When writers describe characters, they often use words with strong connotations to hint at what a character is like, so readers should analyze the writer's choice of words.

READ THE FOLLOWING SENTENCE.

The boy's friends considered him brilliant, but many others considered him merely shrewd.

DETERMINE HOW THE CONNOTATIVE MEANINGS OF THE WORD "SHREWD" AND HOW IT COMPARES WITH THE WORD "BRILLIANT."

Both the words "shrewd" and "brilliant" have a dictionary (denotative) meaning of "sharply intelligent" or "keenly aware." The word "shrewd," however, also has a connotation of cunning or slyness rather than just intelligence. When compared with the word "brilliant," "shrewd" is negative. It connotes a slipperiness that could be associated with a snake. The connotations a word adds to a sentence influence how the reader grasps the meaning; therefore, readers closely should study the words a writer uses. In this instance, the writer has drawn a contrast between positive and negative.

CLUES TO THE SETTING, CHARACTER, AND EVENTS

The words a writer uses to tell a story are of ultimate importance. They give clues to the setting, character, and events. Many words help evoke a sense of time, place, or the setting in which a story takes place. The words suggest the time of day, the time of year, and whether the action takes place a long time ago or in the future. The words also suggest the place where the action occurs by describing items the character sees, uses, or encounters. A writer's words are like the colors a painter uses. A writer's words build one on the other to give the reader a sense of when and where a story occurs.

DETERMINE HOW THE CHOICE OF WORDS IN THE EXCERPT EVOKES A SENSE OF TIME AND PLACE.

Isabel walked through the hall covered with paintings of her ancestors. Down the stairs, she went to the ball room. The dim gas light made everything seem mysterious. She lifted her heavy skirts to ensure she would not fall.

Words can evoke many things. Often they evoke a sense of time and place. The words in the excerpt describe a hall covered with paintings and a ball room. Few homes today have ball rooms. The excerpt talks about having gas light, a certain clue to a time in the past. Isabel lifts her heavy skirts, which also evokes the past and a sense of grandeur. These are just a few examples of how language evokes a sense of time and place. When reading, make sure to take in the descriptions and hints the writer gives about the time and place in which the story occurs.

READ THE FOLLOWING EXCERPT.

> I went to this railroad museum yesterday. It was way cool. I didn't want to leave. I saw loads of model trains. They were running in all sorts of directions. They had hills and tunnels. The streets even had little people.

DETERMINE HOW THE PASSAGE IS AN EXAMPLE OF AN INFORMAL TONE.

The two main styles of writing are formal writing and informal writing. This excerpt is an example of an informal tone, because it makes use of short sentences instead of the longer more complex sentences found in formal writing. The excerpt uses the more casual first person rather than the third person viewpoint, usually used in formal writing. The writer also makes use of colloquial expressions such as "way cool," which formal writers avoid. Another sign of the informal tone is the writer's use of the contraction, "didn't." Formal writing avoids the use of contractions. The expression "loads of" is considered a cliché. Clichés are often used in informal writing, but they are not used in formal style.

PARALLEL PLOTS

Many stories feature parallel plots, or stories within stories, with more than one conflict and more than one main character. These plots are usually related to one another and often add a sense of greater depth than a story with a single plot. While for the most part, short stories are focused on one plot, multiple plots usually are found in novels, most notably in long novels. Some of the most notable examples of parallel plots are found in foreign language books. Russian novels are known for their numerous parallel plots and large numbers of characters. Parallel plots often give a novel a sense of family and history that cannot exist in stories revolving only around one plot.

FLASHBACKS

Flashbacks are a frequently used device especially in movies, but also in short stories and novels. A flashback is a view of something that will happen in the future, and it occurs out of sequence in regard to the chronology of the story's events. For these reasons, flashbacks can have strong effects on literature. They hint at what is to come, and they give the audience or reader an inkling of what might happen. As a result, they easily can create a sense of mystery, tension, or surprise. Generally a story only features one flashback, which often occurs at the beginning of the story. It often sets the stage for conflict that will arise in the narrative. A flashback is one kind of literary device writers use for effect.

PACING

The pacing of a story is its rhythm, which is unique to every story. The pacing is the rate at which a story unfolds or is told. Accordingly, sometimes a story's pacing is slow and leisurely, while at other times it is rapid fire. Writers try to match the pacing of a story with kind of story being told and the characters in the story. A story may start out very slowly and then speed up to a racing rate. The pacing is the heart of a story, and a writer must feel her or his way with it. Variety of pacing is important because it can draw the reader into what is happening. Too much pacing at the same level could become boring. Pacing is the means a writer uses to involve the reader in what happens in the story.

Analyzing Literature from Outside the US

Literature from outside the United States, by its very nature, will contain many different points of views and cultural experiences from those contained in American literature. Characters in books written by people other than Americans may reflect their writers' cultures rather than American culture. As a result, sometimes figuring out exactly what is happening or what an author is attempting to say in a story can prove difficult without some basic knowledge of the writer's culture. One way to discover different viewpoints is to study in what ways a foreign book is different. For instance, Latin American literature often contains references to more cultural turmoil than exists in the United States. Russian literature often infuses a sense of hopelessness into the story, as is the case in Anton Chekov, the great Russian playwright. Characters in Chekov's dramas often face insurmountable problems. Asian literature has a different sense of the importance of the individual than does American literature, as well as a greater sense of respect for tradition and family than is common in American literature.

Discover the cultural differences expressed in the excerpt.

> The three brothers walked through the jungle to a clearing, where they saw a house. They were hungry and tired. They knew the owner was obliged to feed them and let them stay the night, so they knocked at the door.

Many cultural differences in this excerpt affect the story. First, the brothers are walking through the jungle, an experience not part of everyday life in the United States. Also, this passage refers to the house owner's obligation to feed the brothers and invite them to stay the night. These actions represent very different customs than those readily expressed in the United States. As such, a reader might better understand the story if he or she realizes that oftentimes in other countries, people do not have hotels or places to stay other than a person's home. Without this knowledge, the reader may have difficulty comprehending the lesson the writer is trying to teach.

Determine the difference between the way Peter Breughel's Landscape with the Fall of Icarus and W. H. Auden's "Musée des Beaux Arts" interpret and represent the same subject

> The legend of Icarus tells the story of a young man whose father, Daedalus, an inventor, creates wings for Icarus and for himself. He fastens the wings to his son with wax so they can escape from their prison. He then cautions Icarus not to fly too close to the sun because the wax will melt. Icarus does not obey his father, and he falls from the sky. Breughel's painting depicts the scene of Icarus' fall, in which no one is interested enough to stop to observe the tragic death of Icarus. Auden, a poet, saw the painting in the museum mentioned in the poem's title, and in the poem he comments on the apathy people show towards suffering. Breughel's painting is a silent representation of the apathy which Auden verbalizes.

Ways Universal Themes Are Impacted by the Time in Which They Were Written

While universal themes are the same in terms of their meaning and the topics they depict or teach, their presentations are affected by the time in which a literary piece is written. The characters and situations portrayed will mirror the environment in which the writer lived. Ancient literature depicts a time when myth was alive and when the concept of personal freedom still was evolving and not taken for granted. Many Greek plays employ universal themes.

Explain the similarities present in the themes found in "Metamorphoses" by the Latin poet Ovid and the play As You Like It by British playwright William Shakespeare.

> "Metamorphoses," which means transformations or changes, is an epic poem written by Ovid. It details the ways in which nymphs and people are transformed into plants and animals and how springs appear from nowhere. Shakespeare's comedy addresses a similar theme, namely the

way in which people change, although the Shakespearean characters undergo mental changes rather than physical changes. When Shakespeare's characters enter Arden, they practically assume new identities that ultimately allow them to change and grow as people. Both works also address the affect of love on humans and natural human theatrics expressed through song.

EXPLAIN HOW THE MUSICAL WEST SIDE STORY RELATES TO THE SHAKESPEAREAN PLAY ROMEO AND JULIET.

William Shakespeare's tragedy Romeo and Juliet tells the story of a young man and young woman who fall in love, even though their parents are enemies of one another. This play is a tragedy because the young couple dies at the play's conclusion when they fall victim to their parents' warring. The play utilizes dialogue that by today's standards sounds dated and sometimes difficult to understand. The musical *West Side Story* is also about two young people from different cultural backgrounds who fall in love and then die victims of the hatred between Hispanics and Italian-Americans in a poor section of New York City. In the musical, songs and lyrics develop the plot, unlike in Shakespeare's play. The language is modern and the action takes place in a modern world, but the themes are precisely the same.

IMPORTANCE OF BEING ABLE TO READ AND COMPREHEND A WIDE-VARIETY OF TEXTS BY THE END OF GRADE 9

By the time a student completes grade 9, he or she should be able to read and comprehend literature, including stories, dramas, and poetry. Such ability means that the student possesses the basis for furthering his or her ability to go on and read many of the great classics of literature. This ability also will prepare the student for reading even more difficult texts in the next grades. This ability ultimately will lead to a student having a sound background in the cultural aspect of literature and will give the student an excellent background and preparation for whatever the student wishes to pursue in his or her life. Such experience and ability also serves as an aid in developing vocabulary.

Informational Text

FINDING TEXTUAL EVIDENCE

Explicit information is information stated in a text rather than merely hinted at in the text. A nonfiction text typically makes various statements or claims based on supporting details. These statements or claims are explicit, and as such, supporting details need to present accurate evidence. When trying to find textual evidence for explicit material in a text, the reader should look for details that tell about the explicit information and give more information. The supporting information should be based on fact, not opinion. Furthermore, the supporting information should come from a reliable source and be verifiable.

INFERENCE

An inference is a best guess, or the conclusion the reader can make from information in the passage. For instance, if a passage cites studies showing that teenagers need eight hours of sleep per night to do well in school, but also tells how getting to school early interferes with teenagers getting enough sleep, the reader might conclude that teenagers often are tired. While the text does not make this as a direct statement, the reader can figure it out. While the conclusion might be wrong, the reader likely can make the connection as a best guess. When you make an inference, you need to be able to cite the textual evidence upon which the inference is based. In this case, the fact that teenagers are not getting as much sleep as they need because they have to get to school early leads the reader to conclude that teenagers often are tired.

IDENTIFY WHICH INFORMATION IN THE EXCERPT SUPPORTS THE INFERENCE THAT SUGAR CANE NEEDS A HOTTER CLIMATE THAN SUGAR BEETS.

> Sugar cane resembles a tall grass; it needs hot sun and rain to thrive. The cane fills with a dark green juice. Sugar is made from the juice. Sugar beets do not need a lot of heat or rain. The sugar also is made from juice from the beets.

The passage states that sugar cane needs hot sun and rain to thrive supports the inference that sugar cane needs a hotter climate in which to grow than do sugar beets. Another supporting detail is that sugar beets do not need a lot of heat or rain to grow. Since the excerpt states as such, this explicit evidence supports the inference or conclusion. The other details explain the process of obtaining the juice from the two plants, which is then made into sugar, but they do not give details about the right climate for the plants. An inference is the best conclusion a reader can make based on the information given.

DETERMINING THE CENTRAL IDEA OF A PASSAGE

The central idea of a passage is what the passage is mostly about. It is the main point of the passage. Sometimes a passage states the main idea. In such passages, the main idea can be found in a topic sentence at the beginning of the passage or somewhere in the text. Sometimes the main idea is found in the conclusion of a passage. Oftentimes, however, the passage does not state the main idea outright. Instead, the reader needs to figure it out from the information or supporting details found in the passage. The main idea will become more and more evident as a person reads a passage. Most of the time, the main idea does not become evident until the reader has reached nearly the end of the passage. The central or main idea becomes evident as the reader encounters more details and information about the main idea. The details shape the main idea.

DISCUSS WHY THE MAIN IDEA OF THIS EXCERPT IS "THE IRISH HAVE A LONG HISTORY."

> The Irish people of today descended from the three sons of Milesius, the king of Hispania, now known as Spain. They invaded Ireland a thousand years before Christ and intermarried with the local natives, known as the Tuatha De Danaan, who are said to have descended from the Irish goddess Danu.

The information in the excerpt deals the descendants of the Irish people. Furthermore, the passage tells how the three sons of the king of what is now Spain invaded Ireland and married the local natives. The details about the Irish are explicit, accurate facts and can be checked. The central idea emerges from these details. The details tell the early history of the Irish people. Supporting details shape or tell more about the main idea so the reader can tell what a passage is mostly about.

COMPONENTS OF A SUMMARY

A summary of an informational text tells what the text is about and includes some details. It should include the main idea of the passage and the most important supporting details. A summary should be to the point, but also it should include important facts, events, or evidence telling why the text is important or why it was written. Make sure a summary is objective by focusing on the main idea rather than any statements unrelated to the text's main idea. Unlike paraphrasing, a summary is not lengthy and does not include all of the details. It focuses on the most important supporting information to the main idea.

ANALYZING THE AUTHOR'S GOALS AND IDEAS

Every author writes differently, and every type of nonfiction passage has a different goal. The reader's job is to determine the way the author has chosen to present his or her goals and ideas. When you read, you need to ask yourself whether the ideas are presented in a logical, rhetorical, or persuasive manner. You need to seek to discover the author's goal and analyze the way in which the author makes his or her points. You also need to analyze whether the points an author makes seem valid by looking for supporting evidence or reliable and based on fact rather than on opinion.

CONNECTING THE IDEAS IN A NONFICTION PASSAGE

Not only do nonfiction passages have main ideas, but they also have details. Oftentimes these details are supporting details. The reader's job is to understand how these details relate to one another and to the main idea. A careful reader will analyze the author's intent and then consider the author's ideas to see where they lead. The connected ideas form a trail through the text leading to the conclusion. Readers should evaluate the ideas individually to see if they are sound and based on fact rather than opinion. Connecting ideas is the essence of a nonfiction passage.

CONTEXT CLUES

Oftentimes the meaning of unknown words and phrases can be grasped from the context of the sentence in which they are used or from the sentences immediately before or after the unknown words or phrases. Occasionally, in the case of a technical document, reading the entire passage may be necessary in order to understand the meaning of certain technical terms. Words and phrases used in a figurative manner rather than in a literal manner can be difficult to understand without understanding the context of an entire passage. Idioms also can prove difficult to understand and need to be studied in terms of the context of the text for comprehension.

DETERMINE THE KIND OF LANGUAGE AND TONE USED IN THE FOLLOWING COURT RULING.

> "... the prosecution may not use statements, whether exculpatory or inculpatory, stemming from custodial interrogation of the defendant unless it demonstrates the use of procedural safeguards effective to secure the privilege against self-incrimination." (Miranda v. Arizona, 1966)

The language in the court ruling is very formal and technical. It relies on many words drawn from Latin roots, a common language used by lawyers in the courtroom. The key words "exculpatory" and "inculpatory" both derive from the Latin root word "culpa," which means "blame." The prefix "ex-" means "out of" while the prefix "in-" means the opposite. The words mean "cleared of blame" and "blamed" or "incriminated." "Interrogation" also comes from a Latin word meaning "asking" and is defined as "examination by official questioning." "Custodial" is the adjective form of "custody" and means "related to the work of guarding." The word "incrimination" contains the simpler word "crime" and points to the meaning "to cause to appear guilty." The affect of such language makes the court ruling extremely formal and technical.

DETERMINE THE LANGUAGE AND TONE OF THIS NEWSPAPER ARTICLE.

> American Neil Armstrong has become the first man to walk on the Moon.
>
> The astronaut stepped onto the Moon's surface...after first opening the hatch on the Eagle landing craft.
>
> As he put his left foot down first Armstrong declared: "That's one small step for man, one giant leap for mankind."

The excerpt, written July 21, 1969, by the BBC after the Apollo 11 Mission landed on the surface of the moon, shares several attributes with common journalistic language. Paragraphs are short, usually just one or two sentences. The most important facts come first. The basic questions: who, what, when, where and why form the core of the writing. Information is exact. Quotation marks are used in exact wording. The language is easy to comprehend, avoiding any words that the average reader would find difficult to understand. The tone is factual and objective, without any opinion.

READ THE FOLLOWING EXCERPT AND EXPLAIN ITS MEANING.

> To qualify for Social Security disability benefits, first you must have worked in jobs covered by Social Security. Next, you must have a medical condition that meets Social Security's definition of disability. In general, we pay monthly cash benefits to people who are unable to work for a year or more because of a disability.

The passage covers the two criteria necessary to obtain disability benefits from the Social Security Administration. First, you must have worked in a job and paid social security taxes. It is inferred, therefore, that some jobs are not eligible. Secondly, the information states that your medical condition must be one that Social Security covers, so, again, some medical conditions might be ineligible. Once you have satisfied the two conditions, then you will begin receiving money on a monthly basis from Social Security. However, the information also says you have to have been out of work because of disability for at least a year. In order to understand the excerpt, you would have to understand some of the technical language. You would have to figure out what *disability* means. You would have to figure out what is meant by *medical condition*. Another technical expression is *cash benefits.*

FIGURATIVE LANGUAGE.

Figurative language is the use of ordinary language in a non-literal way or non-traditional manner. A writer uses figurative language to expand his or her vision by interjecting images into their writing to make it more colorful and fresh. The literal meaning of a word or phrase is bypassed and a non-literal meaning is attached to it. Further, various kinds of figurative language exist. A simile compares two things using the words *as* or *like.* For example, "His heart was as good as gold." A metaphor compares two things without using the comparing words: "He had a heart of gold." Personification gives a thing or animal human traits, for example, "His heart spoke to me." When reading, look for non-traditional ways of using language for hints to the meaning of the passage.

WHAT KIND OF FIGURATIVE LANGUAGE DOES THIS EXCERPT USE?

> Samantha often thought her kid brother had a brain the size of a pea.

This is an example of a figure of speech called a hyperbole or an exaggeration. This figure of speech is used to create an effect on the reader or to make a point. In this case the wording emphasizes that she thought her kid brother was really dumb and must have a tiny brain. Hyperboles often add a touch of humor to writing and can be found in everyday writing as well as in fiction and poetry. Such language is not meant to be taken literally. This extreme exaggeration differentiates a hyperbole from a metaphor. This example is not personification because it does not attach a human characteristic to an object or an animal.

DENOTATIVE AND CONNOTATIVE MEANINGS OF WORDS

The denotative meaning of a word is the literal definition of a word that often can be found in a dictionary. The connotative meaning is somewhat more subtle; it may also be listed in a dictionary, but this listing will occur after the literal meaning. The connotative meaning is suggested by the word. It is not stated outright, but its usage has established its more hidden meaning. For instance, the words "hefty" and "obese" both mean fat, but obese has the connotation of being unhealthily fat, while hefty is a gentler description and means somewhat fatter than usual. When reading texts, it is a good idea to notice any words with strong connotations, since these words are a key to the author's opinion or point of view.

READ THE FOLLOWING.

> Her mother told her she was too skinny, but Jennifer always felt that she was really slender.

EXPLAIN THE CONNOTATIVE MEANINGS OF THE WORD "SKINNY" AND HOW IT COMPARES WITH THE WORD "SLENDER."

Both the words "skinny" and "slender" can be defined as "thin" or "lean." The word "skinny" has a certain air of unattractiveness about it, while the word "slender" connotes gracefulness, even an air of stylish vogue, so Jennifer and her mother definitely have a different viewpoint. When writing, choose words carefully so you don't depict something in a negative way, when you really mean to depict it in a positive light. Utilize the dictionary for help when choosing words. Furthermore, the thesaurus is useful for listing different connotations of synonyms. By following these suggestions, your words will project exactly what you want to say to your readers. In the same way, check a text for words that have negative or positive connotations. These words are a clue to what a writer thinks about a person or situation.

HOW AN AUTHOR'S IDEAS OR CLAIMS CAN BE DEVELOPED AND REFINED

When authors write a passage, they choose from a variety of ways to bring the reader their ideas or claims. The author must decide how best to present and develop the material and ideas, sometimes including creating sentences, paragraphs, or even larger portions of a text dedicated to the development of one idea. A complicated idea may require a large segment of a text, while some simple ideas could be explained in a single sentence. Oftentimes authors will use subheads to create a clearer focus for the reader to look quickly look through the subheads and determine the location of information. This method way of organizing allows the author to explain several different topics in one passage and helps organize the material as well. When reading, look at the ways in which the author structures his or her ideas.

DETERMINE WHY IT WOULD BE USEFUL FOR HER TO USE SUBHEADS.

> Leslie is working on a report on the destruction of the rainforests. She wants to include information on various aspects of why the destruction is happening and the effect of such destruction on nature and wildlife.

Subheads are an excellent way to organize material and provide the reader with a quick idea of the passage's main content. In a nonfiction passage, often many ideas need to be explored, explained, and developed. To keep them from competing with one another and to keep a reader from becoming confused, subheads can help organize a lot of information that could be lost if lumped under one broad title. Subheads also allow a writer to deviate slightly from the overall main idea so the writer can explain in more depth about one aspect of a topic.

DETERMINING AN AUTHOR'S POINT OF VIEW

The author's point of view is not always immediately evident. Although stated clearly in many texts, often the main point of view is hidden. In such situations, the reader needs to discover through attention to the author's word choice. It is important to read a text closely to figure out what an author thinks about an event, person, topic or issue. When reading, always check for any emotional statements that give hints about the author's feelings. Some authors make their opinions and viewpoints clear when they embrace the use of rhetoric. Rhetoric is effective speaking and persuasion through the use of strong and fresh language meant to sway an audience. Rhetoric can be effective, and the reader may not be aware of how much it is influencing him or her. For this reason, readers should analyze texts for persuasive techniques. A reader needs to know the author's viewpoint before the reader can decide on her or his own.

DISCUSS THE PURPOSE OF RHETORIC IN THE FOLLOWING PASSAGE.

> "He that would make his own liberty secure, must guard even his enemy from oppression; for if he violates this duty, he establishes a precedent which will reach to himself." Thomas Paine, 1795

The excerpt, written by Thomas Paine, one of the Founding Fathers of the United States, uses rhetoric to advance his argument that one sometimes must do what does not come naturally, i.e. protect your enemy, or you yourself may one day be in danger. This passage is meant to make the reader think about liberty. Rhetoric is an oratorical device and a means of persuading an audience. Rhetoric is applicable to both logic and politics. It uses language to create an effect, and it also uses that language to create a more lasting image that is easily recalled afterwards. Rhetoric uses words to motivate actions by others.

DETAILS OF A PERSON'S LIFE MIGHT BE EMPHASIZED IN A MOVIE THAT WOULD NOT BE EMPHASIZED AS MUCH IN A WRITTEN BIOGRAPHY

A movie is a visual medium; a book is a written medium. A person's life would be visualized in a movie in a way it could not be visualized in a book. Primarily, the person playing the subject would act in a certain way that might not be discussed in a written account. For instance, the way a person wears her or his hair, or the way a person walks and talks are not details that a book could describe as successfully. Other details that would be more evident in a movie version of someone's life are the small reactions to events or people that might be omitted from a written account. Much difference exists between the two media; the movie would tend to be more dramatic than the book, as well.

EVIDENCE BASED CLAIMS

Authors often make claims, but it is important that these claims are backed with evidence. This evidence, however, must come from valid sources in order to be accepted. Sources include books written by experts on a subject, information from accredited studies, and trustworthy Internet sources. When analyzing a source, ask yourself if evidence exists asserting the source as an authority on the subject at hand. When reviewing an author's statements, see if reliable sources for the statements exist. If no such information exists, the statements probably are fallacious.

DISCUSS HOW THE EXCERPT BELOW RELATES TO A COMMON AMERICAN THEME.

> "...Oppressed people cannot remain oppressed forever. The yearning for freedom eventually manifests itself, and that is what has happened to the American Negro. Something within has reminded him of his birthright of freedom, and something without has reminded him that it can be gained. Consciously or unconsciously, he has been caught up by the Zeitgeist..."

This excerpt is taken from Martin Luther King, Jr.'s, *Letter from Birmingham Jail,* 1963. Arrested for taking part in a non-violent protest against racial injustice, King wrote the letter to affirm his belief only non-violent protest would help African Americans achieve civil rights. It immediately had a significant impact by starting a dialogue between blacks and whites. The theme of freedom for all people has been the bedrock of American political thought since the country's founding. Civil disobedience was justified, according to Dr. King, because the existing laws were unjust. "Zeitgeist" means "spirit of the times" in German, and refers to the cultural, ethical, and political climate is prevalent at the time.

IMPORTANCE OF BECOMING A PROFICIENT READER OF LITERARY NONFICTION TEXTS BY GRADE 9

By the end of grade 9, a student should be proficient in reading nonfiction texts since the texts that the student will have to comprehend in the next years of high school will be more difficult. These texts contain information on a variety of subjects a student needs to master. Without the ability to read competently, a student will have a deficit in his or her education. Reading comprehension is important for all walks of life, whether academic or not. The ability to read with comprehension is especially important for high school success.

Writing

Producing Clear and Coherent Writing

Each genre of writing requires its own traits, but to attain clear and coherent writing it is necessary to plan what you will be writing. First, decide on your goal, or whether you are trying to inform, persuade, or entertain. With your goal in mind, you need to organize your material if you are writing a nonfiction piece. You need to have a clear idea of your main ideas and supporting details. If you are planning to write a narrative, you need to pay attention to developing your story in a clear and flowing manner. Then, create characters through skillful use of description, dialogue, and action. In addition in all types of writing you need to establish a tone. You also need to make sure your writing is free of grammatical or spelling errors. Close rereading and editing is part of the writing process, as well.

Importance of Planning, Revising, Editing, and Reviewing a Text to Make It Reach a Specific Audience

When beginning to write, you should develop a plan about what you want to discuss and the points you want to make. An outline can prove helpful if you are writing a nonfiction piece. If you are writing a narrative, you might want to make a story map. Next, you should write a first draft. Once you have finished the writing, you should put it aside for a time. When you come back to it, you will see it with fresh eyes and will see more easily what needs to be changed or revised. After you make the revisions and put the writing aside again, then reread the writing and begin to edit it for any grammatical, spelling, punctuation, or usage errors. Make sure that the supporting details are clear and in a logical order in a report. Rework the dialogue to make it more precise in a story. Read your work to someone else and ask for feedback. Finally, revise it again.

Read the Following Passage, Explain Why It Needs Revision, and Tell How to Revise It.

> Learning how to play lacrosse is too hard. Everyone knows lacrosse was invented by the Indians. But let me tell you it is a cool game. It's played with a stick that hits a ball that goes into an opponent's net for a goal. And it move's fast.

The writer of the passage has not made clear what she is trying to communicate. The passage is unorganized, and it contains grammatical errors, usage errors, and clichés.

Here Is a Revision That Reads Much Better:

> Lacrosse, a sport originated by Native Americans, is a fast-moving game played with a lacrosse stick and a small, hard rubber ball. The object of the game is to use the stick to get the ball into the opponent's net and score a goal. It is not an easy game, but it is enjoyable.

Here, the writer has organized her thoughts in a logical order. The writing has a definite statement (*lacrosse is a fast-moving game)* and tells about the object of the game (*get the ball into the opponent's net).* It also includes the writer's feelings about the game as a conclusion. Everything now makes sense and the passage is free of grammatical and usage errors.

Using the Internet

Online sources are a wonderful tool for writers. They can get works published at little or no cost either as an e-book or a printed book. There are other options available as well, such as editing and marketing services offered on many Internet sites. Writing tools give help with everything from style to grammar. Many sites are reliable research possibilities and provide accurate and objective information. Make sure to pick reliable sources for any research. Also, be sure to cite Internet sources using an accepted format such as that from the MLA (Modern Language Association). Many sites allow people to work together on projects regardless of their physical location. Chat rooms and topic websites are other tools that allow exchanges of information and have shared writing projects.

Conducting a Short Research Project

A plan of action is a good first step when conducting a short or a sustained research project to answer a question or solve a problem. Before you go online, make a list of key words relating to the question or problem. Utilize these words either in a search engine or an online or print encyclopedia. You can consult many sources to find the information you are seeking. Back issues of magazines, journals, and newspapers also can be of use. Meet your objective by finding an answer to a question or a solution to a problem. Use information from many sources and then synthesize it so the writing flows logically. Show that you have a good grasp of the subject and what it encompasses.

Make an outline including the kind of information you are seeking as well as the scope of the project. Then make a list of pertinent keywords to search for the topic in multiple print and digital sources. Take notes and make an outline of the similarities as well as the differences you encounter in various sources. Journals, text books, magazines, and newspapers are of use; the number of sources you can uncover is limitless. Whatever the source, verify its timeliness, accuracy, and credibility. Dismiss any sources that seem questionable. When recording the information, make sure to use fresh language and not copy anything directly except for quotations cited appropriately to avoid plagiarism. Use the Modern Language Association (MLA) guidelines for all citations.

Analyze how Tom Stoppard used a Shakespearean play for the basis of his play Rosenkrantz & Guildenstern Are Dead.

Stoppard's play *Rosenkrantz & Guildenstern Are Dead* is a mirror image of Shakespeare's *Hamlet*. In Stoppard's play, Rosenkrantz and Guildenstern are the main characters. They portray schoolmates who wander around aimlessly, bewildered by the events that take place around them, and babble nonsense to each other. In *Hamlet,* the two never appeared on stage. In Stoppard's play, these characters come across a theatrical troupe called the Tragedians and find themselves in a performance of *Hamlet*. They are asked to help Prince Hamlet, who may or may not be going insane. The play depicts a searching for values and dismay that nothing is certain. As one character called The Player says, "Uncertainty is the normal state. You're nobody special." Unlike Hamlet, this play is written in modern language, but the two works have similar themes.

Jerry is writing an article about space travel. Evaluate the following sources as to their reliability..

http://www.nasa.gov/home/index.html

Encyclopedia Britannica, 15th edition, © 1986

When doing research, information gathered from print sources often can be just as reliable as information obtained from the Internet. However, when researching space travel, the information included in the Encyclopedia Britannica would be too dated and would be missing important information from 1986 until now. Such an encyclopedia would be reliable if you were researching classical Greek philosophy. For research on space travel, though, the NASA (National Aeronautics and Space Administration) website would be much more reliable and up-to-date. For these reasons, it is important always to check the date on all sources to make sure they contain the latest information so your research will not be outdated.

Writing Routinely

Students should learn to write routinely. Whatever the task or purpose, students need to be able to put their ideas into words. There are various types of writing. A report may take longer to write than a short answer to a question. Students need to learn to pace themselves when writing longer pieces. They should be prepared to write a rough draft and then revise, edit, and revise again. Shorter writing assignments will not require as much attention since their structure is more straight forward. Nonetheless, whether writing short or long pieces, students need to find a way to become communicators with the written word, including employing proper grammar, spelling, and varied syntax in order to keep the reader interested.

Persuasive Text

Introducing a Claim

An excellent way to introduce an argument in a persuasive passage and create an appropriate organization involves ordering your claims and then finding research that supports those claims. A good way to begin is making an outline. Put your claim at the top, and then list the reasons and the evidence supporting the statement. This can be done if you have more than one claim. Include counterclaims and evidence of why you do not think they are correct. When you write the passage, hold the reader's attention by using a strong tone, rhetoric, and fresh language. Be sure to your claims with evidence from acceptable sources. Finally, restating your mail claim at the conclusion of your passage is a good idea.

Providing the Most Relevant Evidence

Whether presenting a claim or a counterclaim, you should include supporting evidence for each one. Even though you are emphasizing your claim, you still need to include reliable information about the counterclaim. Including this information will increase the effectiveness of your argument by presenting both sides. The evidence needs to be reliable and relevant and should cover every point made. You need to do a great deal of research to develop your evidence. While researching, try to anticipate what readers might say; this anticipation will help you develop your claim thoroughly. It is not enough to research a claim on the Internet because many internet sources are dubious at best. Instead, look for objective sites. Find experts that you can quote, and use proven statistics. Give each claim and counterclaim its own paragraph or two. Make sure to present your information in a logical manner so the reader easily can understand.

Creating Cohesion

The best way to create cohesion between claims and evidence is to organize your ideas and then write sentences explaining your reasons and providing evidence that follows your main ideas logically. Careful research will make your argument cohesive and easy to understand. Your claim and evidence should relate clearly to each other. Words indicating to the reader that the claim and evidence are related include: *since, because, as a consequence* or *as a result.* You also can utilize clauses to demonstrate a relationship between the reason and the effect. *As a result of Dr. Long's experiment, more and more people have come to the realization that this new product is flawed.* The first clause sets the tone and establishes causality between the reason and effect. After writing, re-read to verify that relationships between cause and effect are logical.

Maintaining a Formal Style

A formal style is the usual style when writing arguments. This style helps the writer achieve objectivity and keeps the language precise. Formal writing consists of complete sentences; fragments should be avoided unless used for a specific reason. Do not use the first or second person. The third person is standard in formal writing. Use an active voice, which projects more energy, and avoid the passive voice. Do not use contractions and make sure not to change tenses between sentences or paragraphs. Ensure that you use proper spelling and punctuation. Reread and edit your passage several times to improve the language wherever possible. Make sure your ideas follow a logical order, as well.

READ THE FOLLOWING PASSAGE AND SUGGEST HOW TO MAKE IT MORE FORMAL.

> I always like fishing. Even if I don't catch anything. It's just fun being out on the water. I like the quiet and the peacefulness. And nobody is around to bother me. I just row away from the dock, and it's like a whole other world.

HERE IS ONE WAY TO RE-WRITE THE PASSAGE.

> Fishing for pleasure is one of life's great joys, and it has been a popular pastime for centuries. Fishing allows one to relax, enjoy fresh air and sunshine, and forget about stress and pressure. Fishing develops one's sense of patience; it requires no special skills or training.

Using the third person makes the passage more formal as well as more authoritative. Short simple sentences are replaced with longer, complex sentences, which make the passage more interesting to read. Contractions and clichés are avoided. The vocabulary is more sophisticated. The final result is a text that is informed, precise and finely crafted.

IMPORTANCE OF A CONCLUDING STATEMENT IN A PERSUASIVE PASSAGE

A concluding statement is important for a persuasive passage because it sums up the main points of the passage and gives the reader a sense of completion by bringing the passage to a natural end. The concluding sentence should pull all aspects of the passage together and make sense of all the ideas, evidence, and details included previously. The concluding statement also will be somewhat inspiring since it is the writer's final attempt to convince the reader of his or her standpoint. A good concluding statement serves to cement the bonds the writer has developed with the reader.

WHAT KIND OF ARGUMENT WOULD THE FOLLOWING CONCLUDING SENTENCE BEST CONCLUDE?

> That is why it is important to have regular physical checkups with your doctor.

The sentence would make a good concluding sentence for a passage outlining reasons for seeing a doctor regularly. Such reasons might include that regular physical checkups can disclose conditions that might not be noticed, such as high blood pressure or an irregular heartbeat. Furthermore, a checkup gives the patient a chance to talk to a doctor about any problems that might exist. The doctor could order certain lab tests to check further. This concluding sentence brings all the elements of the argument together.

Informational or Explanatory Text

INTRODUCING A TOPIC

An informational or explanatory text should introduce the topic featured in the text. You can accomplish this by using a topic sentence followed by details supporting your thesis. Another tactic involves referring to a current event, even if your topic refers to something in history. Ideas should be organized in a logical manner, with supporting details coming right after a main concept. Connections can be made between concepts by using connecting words such as *however, since,* and *as a result.* Distinctions between ideas also should be made clear and can be signaled by words and phrases such as *but* or *on the other hand.* Furthermore, you can choose whether to include a specific relationship such as cause and effect, question and answer, or problem and solution.

Using Graphics, Formatting, and Multimedia

There are many ways to present information so it is easier to understand. Graphics are extremely useful because they present detailed information in a manner that is quickly grasped. Instead of putting the information in a paragraph, it can be fashioned into a graphic, which is much more approachable for the reader. Another useful tool is subheadings. Each subhead introduces a new concept or idea in the text and allows the reader to determine the article's main points. Multimedia, including voice over, videos, or even movies, represents another way to present information. Since movies and videos are so much a part of everyday life, most people respond very easily to this kind of presentation. Difficult material can be made much more palatable with these tools.

Developing a Topic

It is important to develop the topic in an informational or explanatory text by utilizing relevant facts that clearly support the main topic. After the introduction of the topic, supporting details should follow, including relevant facts rather than opinions. At times it may be necessary to include definitions for terms that might be unfamiliar to the reader. The cited supporting details should be concrete, which means they come from reliable sources. Quotations by experts in the field also develop the topic, and they make the text more readable and lend it variety. The results of any research also are helpful. Consider using graphics to help readers understand any technical material. Charts, multimedia techniques as well as subheads also can develop the topic.

Creating Cohesion

Appropriate transition words help clarify the relationships between ideas and concepts and create a more cohesive passage. Good writers know that such words and phrases serve to clarify the relationships between ideas and concepts. Words or phrases that show causality between ideas include *consequently, therefore,* and *as a result of. However, on the other hand, in contrast, but,* or *similarly* indicate a compare and contrast relationship. When examples of different concepts are used, words such *as namely, for example,* or *for instance* act as transition words. When it is necessary to show the order of importance of ideas or concepts, transition words such as *at first, primarily, secondly, former,* or *latter* can be used.

How could the following sentences be written with a better transition between the ideas?

They didn't know what they were doing. The boat often ran aground.

Rewriting the two sentences requires understanding the sentences' relationships with each other. In this passage, causality is suggested. The boat ran aground because they didn't know what they were doing. To combine the sentences, you need to use an appropriate transition word. This case has several options. The phrase "as a result" works well. It shows the causality between the two thoughts: "They didn't know what they were doing; as a result, the boat often ran aground." Other causality words include *because, consequently,* or *therefore.* The two sentences could be joined with any of those words, and the combination would make more sense than the separate sentences.

Using Precise Language

Writers of informational or explanatory texts must use precise language and domain-specific vocabulary in order to accurately communicate their ideas. General vocabulary words will not assert the necessary points. The reader will not follow the main idea of the passage if it lacks details supplied by carefully chosen, precise, and domain-specific language. For instance, using the term *renal* in a in a medical text is more technical than the term *kidney*. While researching a subject, you should include technical vocabulary to use during the writing of the text. Oftentimes it may be necessary to define domain-specific words for the reader.

Maintain a Formal Style

Writers of informative or explanatory passages generally use a formal style because it lends greater credence and a sense of more objectivity to the passage. The use of an informal or colloquial tone is frowned upon. Likewise, such passages generally use the third person for objectivity. Good writers use complex sentences, which are longer and add a further tone of formality and depth to the subject. By using a formal style, good writers show the seriousness of the subject; formal writing also includes clear and well-grounded supporting details. Personal opinion rarely has a place in an informative or explanatory passage, unless justified in some acceptable way.

Tell why the following excerpt is an example of a formal style.

> "Alas! the grand style is the last matter in the world for verbal definition to deal with adequately. One may say of it as is said of faith: 'One must feel it in order to know what it is.'"
>
> (Matthew Arnold, "Last Words on Translating Homer," 1873)

Matthew Arnold, a poet, commented on the "grand style," by which he means very formal writing. In so doing, he gives a good example of formal writing. Arnold uses the third person to approach his subject. He also uses precise language. His vocabulary is not simple; instead, it is on a high level. He uses the active voice rather than the passive voice. He also employs some drama, when he opens his piece with "Alas." He also tells his audience that defining the "grand style" is not an easy manner, but it can be sensed.

Having an Effective Conclusion

While a good beginning is essential, equally important to an essay, lecture, or other presentation is an effective conclusion. A good concluding statement should sum up the overall intention of the text and serve to "wrap up" the presentation so the reader is aware that you have made a logical ending to your thesis and has closure. Ideally the conclusion would review the most important points made in the presentation, the reasoning employed, and the supporting arguments for this reasoning. The conclusion builds a bridge between the presentation and the audience that helps to reassert the importance of the effort and impact the viewer's memory favorably. A good conclusion allows the reader to sit back and weigh the overall impact of the presentation.

Narratives

Establishing a Point of View

To set the stage for a narrative, introduce the reader to the setting and the characters. Next, introduce a plot line, consisting of various events that lead to a problem, climax, and resolution. This gives a narrative structure. The way the author introduces these elements is important in demonstrating the effectiveness of the narrative. Make sure to use language to describe the setting and characters so they grab the reader's interest. Make the details specific. Such a conclusion or resolution ties up the details of the story.

Introducing Characters

An author introduces characters to the reader through many means. Some authors use a description to introduce a character; other authors use an event or action to introduce a character. Still others introduce a character through the character's dialogue. In all cases, the reader receives his first impression of a character with the introduction. The reader may read a description of a character and get a sense of not only the character's appearance, but also the character's feelings. Having a character react to something also tells about a character's personality. What the character says certainly will leave an impression on the reader. Readers will be startled, amused, and saddened by characters because of their words and actions, and how the author describes them.

DETERMINE ANNA'S PROBLEM.

> Anna looked down at her hands. They were trembling. This was the third interview this week, but so far there were no job offers. Since Ted had lost his job, money was very tight. She was their only hope. When the interviewer asked her name, Anna could not speak.

Anna is nervous. We know this because her hands were trembling. She is apprehensive. The reader can tell this because this was the third job interview Anna had been on in a week, and she did not have any offers. Ted, who may be her husband, is out of work. They have very little money. She feels she is the only hope they have. The author has described Anna's problem through the words he uses and the hints he makes. Anna's problem is that she needs a job, but she can't seem to find one. Her situation is even worse because her nervousness makes her unable to speak to the interviewer.

TECHNIQUES USED BY AN AUTHOR

Authors use a variety of techniques to bring to life their narratives. Authors employ dialogue to help develop characters. The words characters speak give endless clues into their personalities as well as their conflicts and needs. Dialogue also gives the reader a sense of what is happening. Pacing is another valuable technique. Rather than have the action move along at the same pace, writers change pace according to the effect they want to achieve. To build mystery or drama, a fast pace works well; a slow pace often sets the stage before something eventful occurs. Pace is the rhythm of a narrative. Plot lines are equally important, because they provide structure in the narrative. Description can create a setting or give insight into characters. They help the reader visualize what is happening.

CREATING A COHERENT SEQUENCE OF EVENTS

A narrative's sequence of events usually emerges in order, because this is the most straightforward way to create a coherent sequence, which will not leave the reader confused. Such a structure provides a natural flow in the narrative, revealed through the dialogue and plot. A coherent sequence enhances a story, and it should never seem forced or unnatural. On the other hand, some writers change the natural order with a literary device called flashback. A flashback occurs when the writer chooses to go forward in time and then follow the natural sequence. Properly done, the flashback makes sense in the context of the story. Flashbacks can add a sense of mystery or suspense to a narrative as well as provide the reader with another literary device, foreshadowing. Nonetheless, chronological narration is used more frequently.

USING PRECISE LANGUAGE

Precise language is essential to a narrative so the story will come alive to the reader. Precise language including phrases and sensory language helps the reader imagine a place, situation, or person in the way the writer wishes. Through his or her words, the writer shapes the action of the story. Precise language should be included in the dialogue since it tells so much about the characters in a story. Sensory language can add extra detail, feeling, and color. Sensory language also appeals to the senses, so it creates a strong bond between the story and the reader.

READ THE EXCERPT.

> In the cool blue twilight of two steep streets in Camden Town, the shop at the corner, a confectioner's, glowed like the butt of a cigar.

Analyze the precise language used in this opening line from "The Invisible Man" by G. K. Chesterton.

This opening line is filled with precise and sensory language. The description of the "blue twilight" of two "steep" streets creates an image of a growing darkness in the streets. Here the author uses a metaphor to add color to his writing. The image of the shop that "glowed like the butt of a cigar" brings up a strong image of what the shop looked like, shining in the dark. The passage seems to suggest that only this shop was lit up. In this case, the author uses a simile comparing the shop to a lit cigar. This language draws the reader immediately into the story and leaves the reader wanting to see where the story goes from there.

Role of the Conclusion

As a reader's last experience with a story, a narrative's conclusion tells the most telling of all events in a story. The sense of finality in a good conclusion generally leaves the reader satisfied. Nonetheless, much of modern literature does not leave the reader satisfied, since the writer intends to leave the reader wondering what will happen next. Some writers, however, do not intend to conclude in such a way and still confuse the reader with an inadequate ending that does not relate to the events occurring in a narrative. A bad conclusion fails to resolve the conflict in the story; a good conclusion resolves the conflict even if the resolution is not one that the reader might prefer.

Vladimir is writing a short story about a trip he made last summer to visit his grandmother in Chicago. He has written about his preparations, the trip, and the things he did with his grandmother. He is looking for a conclusion to the story. Describe what Vladimir should look for in writing a conclusion.

Vladimir should write a conclusion tying all the elements of the story together. Since he went on a trip to visit his grandmother, his short story should end with what happened when the trip ended. Such a conclusion would be the most obvious choice. Vladimir would bring the story to its close with a good ending so the reader could know what happened and what it meant to him. In this way, the reader would not be left with many questions at the end. The story's opening and its events all lead up to this point. With the addition of a good conclusion, Vladimir's story would be well crafted.

Speaking and Listening

Discussions

Preparing for a Group Discussion

A good group discussion leads to interactive learning and increases self-confidence. Careful reading of the assigned text material is important. Go over it as many times as necessary until you have a thorough understanding. Class discussions can be valuable since they promote dialogue between you and your classmates, and they also prepare you for adult life, where effective communication is essential. Think ahead of time of interpretive questions, or questions that have more than one answer. They will contribute to a lively discussion. Practice being a good listener. During the discussion, try to avoid any conflict, since conflict generally kills the discussion.

Collegial Discussions

In well-organized collegial discussions, all students should participate actively, both listening as well as speaking. A reference such as *Robert's Rules of Order* can be quite helpful. One or two students should be appointed leader. All of the students should feel free to disagree, question, or admit when they don't understand something. Interruptions should not be allowed. It is essential that all students should come to the discussion well prepared. If disagreement occurs, the leader(s) should mediate until a consensus can be reached and facilitate the process until voting on any key issues can begin.

Questions that can be answered simply "yes" or "no" will not result in a good discussion, nor will any of the participants gain anything. Asking a question such as, "Can you give me an example?" or "What did you mean when you said...?"encourages a response which helps other students think about a subject and therefore learn. This type of communication is known as Socratic questioning, from the Greek philosopher Socrates. Questions should seek clarification, probe assumptions, probe implications, and seek clarification. The discussion moves along and the group can think about the subject, put the information together meaningfully, and create new ideas.

Class discussion guidelines should stress that everyone should be treated with respect. Whoever is leading the discussion needs to assume that everyone present has something to contribute to the discussion. No one should worry that they may say the wrong thing. Everyone should be able to understand and think critically about the assigned topic; if someone is confused, they should state the source of their confusion. Taking notes during the discussion can help you remember a point that you want to bring up later. Ideas can be challenged without resorting to personal attacks.

Responding to Diverse Perspectives

Every group is diverse in its own way. The opinions of others need to be respected. Perhaps in a discussion someone will bring up a perspective you had not thought of before. This perspective might help you see things differently, and you might reach a new conclusion. It is, therefore, most important that all participants listen carefully to what everyone is saying. In any discussion, the dialogue should be respectful and free of any emotional outbursts. Each participant in the group should be able to identify points of agreement and disagreement.

Intergrating Various Sources of Information

Students must be capable of using digital media. Accordingly, he or she should be able to able to answer questions that arise with visual, quantitative, or verbal methods. Whether researching information from print sources or on the Internet, it is imperative to verify the credibility and accuracy of the information. Ask questions such as, "Can the author be connected to the subject? What are the author's qualifications, and what organizations or associations is the author connected to? Can supporting evidence be documented. Is the information current? A scholarly site, where the content is peer reviewed, is much more authoritative than an *ezine*, in which anyone can write.

Analyzing a Speaker's Point of View

The ability to analyze a speaker's point of view is an important skill, and will be important in adult life. First, examine the objective of the speech. Then, consider if the speaker comes across as knowledgeable. Examine whether the use of evidence seems logical and credible. Attempt to judge the quality of the evidence, and how clearly that evidence is presented. A good speaker uses rhetoric to persuade the audience. Faulty reasoning arises from the lack of any common sense. Ask yourself if the speaker appears dogmatic or opinionated, or if he/she is clearly and demonstrably open-minded.

Presentations

Presenting Evidence That Is Relevant and Credible

A good presentation of information should have a logical flow. It makes concrete statements rather than abstractions. Furthermore, one would present information differently to an audience of ten than to an audience of 100. Make the information useful and focused. Evidence should be relevant and supported with quotes, examples, and statistics from credible sources. Cite sources, and make sure that they are current. Important points can be repeated for effect. Using graphics at appropriate times will reinforce the argument(s) you are making. You should practice making your presentation with friends or family and listen to their critiques.

Using Digital Media to Enhance the Presentation

We live in a world of rapid change, and we need to use new tools to produce effective presentations. Electronic presentations will become the norm. Web-based presentation tools can promote your audience to think visually with diagrams, charts, and maps. They also keep an audience interested and develop your reasoning and evidence. Cloud-based applications such as Prezi are replacing the standard slide show. Adding animation and music with software such as Adobe Flash greatly enhances a presentation and makes the content more memorable. As with any other presentation, it is best to practice a few times so everything flows smoothly.

Adapting Speech to a Variety of Contexts

English is a language of nuances, or subtle differences in meaning. As such, many synonyms can be utilized to attain the exact meaning you are trying to communicate, so using a thesaurus and dictionary when writing your presentation can be helpful. However, it is important that you use correct grammar and language. Maintain eye contact with the audience; if you stare off into space, your audience will lose interest quickly. Some people find it useful to begin a presentation with a joke. Whatever your style, you should project confidence and knowledge of your subject. Try your presentation out before a friend first and ask for his or her response.

Determine Why This Sentence Should Be Rewritten

They like to sail, skiing, and they also hike too.

This sentence is not in a parallel form. Instead, it is an example of faulty parallelism, since it has three different verb forms. All the verb forms in the sentence should be the same. The first verb, to sail, is an infinitive. The second is in a gerund form; the third is in present tense form. The sentence should be written so all the verbs agree: "They like to sail, to ski, and to hike, too. Now all of the verbs are in an infinitive form. Another way to write the sentence is: "They like sailing, skiing, and hiking." Now all the verbs are in a gerund form. Good writers make sure to check that their text does not contain faulty parallelism.

Language

Parallel Construction

When writing a series of words in the same form or describing the same thing, they should be in the same grammatical form. For instance, if you are using more than one verb in a sentence, the verbs must be in the same form. Also, if you are listing nouns, they must all be in the same form. The following sentence is an example of faulty parallelism, since the description of the lake is not in a parallel form. "The lake is choppy today, and it has much mud." This should be written, "The lake is choppy and muddy today," so the adjectives are parallel.

Identify and discuss the underlined phrase in the following sentence.

Their throats parched by the searing heat, the firefighters battled the blaze.

The phrase "throats parched by the searing heat" is an absolute phrase since the noun "throats" is modified by a participle phrase "parched by the searing heat" and has no relationship to the rest of the sentence, which means it does not modify anything in the main clause. The participle "being" is understood rather than stated here; the sentence could be written "Their throats being parched by the searing heat" but "being" is more commonly not stated. There are a large number of phrases other than absolute phrases; they include noun, verb, adjectival, adverbial, participial, and prepositional.

Determine the kinds of clauses found in the following sentence.

After magna hardens, it forms igneous rocks, which consist of extrusive and intrusive rocks.

This sentence contains three clauses in all. The first is "After magna hardens." This is an adverb clause because it tells when something happens. Also, it is a subordinate clause and depends on the next clause: "it forms igneous rocks." This clause is an independent clause. It can stand on its own as a sentence. The next clause "which consist of extrusive and intrusive rocks" is also a dependent clause. It cannot stand alone, because it depends on the independent clause. It is a relative clause because it tells something about the magna. Other kinds of clauses include adjective clauses and noun clauses.

Use of a Semi-colon When Linking Two Independent Clauses

Two independent clauses can be joined by placing a semi-colon between the two clauses and frequently adding a conjunctive adverb. For instance, these independent clauses could be joined in the following manner.

One way to join these clauses is:

Jan's cell phone is new; it doesn't work very well.

However, a better way to join the clauses and clarify the relationship between them is by adding the conjunctive adverb however.

Jan's cell phone is new; however, it doesn't work very well.

There are many conjunctive adverbs, including nevertheless, still, though, also, furthermore, equally, likewise, consequently, therefore, so, and thus.

Rules for Using Colons for Lists or Quotations

Colons are used at the start of a list of items, as in the following.

My grandfather's garden has the following flowers: pansies, roses, camellias, peonies, tulips, and marigolds.

However, if the list immediately follows a verb or a preposition do not use a colon.

My grandfather's garden contains flowers *such as* pansies, roses, camellias, peonies, tulips, and marigolds.

Use a colon to introduce a long or formal quotation. A formal quotation is often preceded by such words as *these, the following*, or as *follows.*

"The Rime of the Ancient Mariner" contains this stanza:

Water, water, everywhere,

And all the boards did shrink;

Water, water, everywhere

Nor any drop to drink

Correct the spelling in the sentence below.

The chorus was barely audable over the sound of the car engine, but no one seemed aggrevated by it even though it continued throughout the performence.

The incorrectly spelled words are "audable," which should be spelled "audible;" "aggrevated," which is spelled "aggravated;" and "performance," which is spelled "performance." It is important to know how to spell words correctly. One good tool is sounding out words by breaking them into syllables. Check a word for familiar affixes. Use a dictionary to make sure you know how to spell a word. Keep word lists and use each word in a sentence. Practice with a few words at a time. Spelling rules can help as well. "I before e except after c," (receive) is one rule. Others are "drop the final e" (like, liking) and "double the last consonant" (stop, stopped) when added suffixes.

Importance of Using Style Manuals

When you write a report, story, essay, or persuasive text, you need to follow guidelines so your writing conforms to the appropriate guidelines. Two excellent sources are the *MLA (Modern Language Association) Handbook* and Turabian's *Manual for Writers.* The *MLA Handbook* is used by universities, colleges, and secondary schools as the best reference for writing a research paper. The guide gives advice on all aspects of writing research papers, from picking a topic to submitting the paper. Kate Turabian's *A Manual for Writers of Term Papers, Theses, and Dissertations* is also valuable and gives information about all aspects of writing research papers from citing sources to determining the difference between primary and secondary sources.

Rewrite the following passage so it is grammatically correct.

The title of Steinbeck's The Grapes of Wrath comes from a line in the first verse of the Battle Hymn of the Republic "He is trampling down the vintage where the grapes' of wrath are stored.

THE SENTENCE SHOULD BE WRITTEN THIS WAY:

> The title of Steinbeck's *The Grapes of Wrath* comes from a line in the first verse of the "Battle Hymn of the Republic": "He is trampling down the vintage where the grapes of wrath are stored."

The title of the Steinbeck book should be in italics; the name of the hymn should have quotation marks around it. There should be a colon before the quotation. An apostrophe is not needed after the word *grapes* since it is not in a possessive form. Finally, there should be a quotation mark at the end of the quote. These changes follow the guidelines of both the *MLA Handbook* and Turabian's *Manual for Writers.*

USING CONTEXT CLUES

In a sentence containing a new word or phrase, often the sentences before and after it can provide the reader with clues regarding the meaning of the new word or phrase. A reader can often figure out the meaning of an unknown word from these clues. For instance, a passage might say that Vanessa lived in an *affluent* neighborhood. A reader might not be familiar with the word *affluent,* but then the passage goes on to say that the neighborhood was filled with expensive homes, beautifully kept lawns, and at least three cars in the garages of each of these spacious and elegant houses. These facts give clues about the meaning of *affluent.* The reader could realize that *affluent* means rich. Another helpful clue is the placement of the word *affluent* immediately preceding a noun, *neighborhood.* This placement indicates that *affluent* likely is an adjective. As a result, the reader should look for another adjective to describe the neighborhood.

USE CONTEXT CLUES TO DETERMINE THE MEANING OF MOBILIZE IN THE FOLLOWING EXCERPT.

> Dion was determined to *mobilize* his neighbors to keep the local elementary school from closing. He trained volunteers to go to each apartment in their building and get signatures on a petition asking the board of education not to close the school. The school was saved and Dion was the neighborhood hero.

To figure out the meaning of the word *mobilize,* the reader needs to analyze the rest of the sentence as well as the following sentences. It would appear that Dion got his neighbors to take action and that the action worked. He actively trained volunteers, and they obtained signatures on the petition asking that the school not be closed. As a result, the meaning of *mobilize* becomes clearer. It means to *take action*. If you substitute *take action* for *mobilize,* the excerpt makes sense. The fact that *mobilize* is a verb also tells the reader that a synonym also needs to be a verb.

DETERMINE HOW THE CONTEXT CLUES HELP THE READER FIGURE OUT THE MEANING OF THE PHRASE TIED THE KNOT IN THE FOLLOWING EXCERPT.

> Hassan and Aisha *tied the knot* on Saturday, but they decided to postpone their honeymoon for a month. Then they will go to Florida.

While the phrase *tied the knot* might seem to have a nautical or military overtone because of the word *knot,* this is not an accurate understanding. The phrase is actually an idiom, or expression with a meaning unrelated to its literal meaning. However, the sentence containing the phrase in question contains a clue to help the reader figure out that *tied the knot* means *got married.* The clue is the word *honeymoon*, generally taken after a marriage. The reader also can figure out that the phrase's meaning is an action and that a verb would be the correct synonym for the phrase.

HOW CERTAIN ENDINGS CAN INDICATE A WORD'S PART OF SPEECH

You can tell a great deal about a word's form by examining its suffix. Certain suffixes signal that a word is a noun. One such ending is *-tion*; it forms a noun from the stem of the word complete:

completion. Other endings make a stem into an adjective. In this case the addition of *-ed* creates the adjective form of the verb, *completed.* The adverb is formed from the root word, complete with the suffix -ly. It is important to be able to analyze a word, not just for its etymology, but also for its part of speech.

Identify the part of speech of the word contender and how you made this determination.

The root word for *contender* is *contend.* The suffix *-er* indicates that the word is a noun. The suffix -*er* indicates someone who does something, so in this case it means someone who contends. If you know that the word *contend* means *compete* then you can figure out that a contender is someone who competes. If you wanted to do so, you could make the word into an adjective by adding the suffix *-ed.* The noun is formed by removing the *d* from the end of the root word and adding the suffix *-tion: contention.*

Determine the etymology of the word accentuate in the following sentence.

> Ricky liked to *accentuate* his good traits.

Without the presence of context clues in the sentence, you need to look up the word. The etymology of the word helps you discover its meaning. The dictionary says that *accentuate* is a transitive verb, that is, it has an object. This word contains four syllables: ac.cent.u.ate. The word has a Latin origin and comes from the word accentus, which means accent. When you look up the meaning of accent, you find that one of its meanings is to stress or focus attention on something. These clues provide insight into the meaning of accentuate, which means to stress or focus on something.

Using General and Specialized Reference Materials to Find the Pronunciation of a Word

A print or digital dictionary can be used as a means to discover many things about a word. It will show the correct pronunciation of a word, tell its meaning, and its part of speech. It also will tell how the word was derived, or its etymology. The dictionary has a guide that shows how to sound out the words, and lists all the parts of speech a word can be used as and the meanings it has in each form. In addition, this entry will tell you the ancient origins of the word. The thesaurus is an extremely useful tool because it lists synonyms for all the various meanings a word can have, in order to clarify the precise meaning as used in the context of a text. In this way, you can find other words to use in a report or text that mean the same as a certain overused word. Many books will have a glossary to help you with difficult or even technical words used in the text.

Read the next sentence. Figure out the meaning of conventional.

> The group of poets decided that they preferred experimenting with form rather than working in a conventional manner.

Context clues might suggest that *conventional* means usual or normal. But you may not be certain. For this reason, it is a good idea to look up words about which you are unsure in the dictionary. There you will find all the meanings of a word, and you can verify your own understanding of the word. In the dictionary there are various meanings of the word, but one seems closest to the meaning you have come up with. That meaning is "conforming to established practice or accepted standards." This meaning fits with the context of the sentence, so you have verified your understanding of the word.

Define the terms *Euphemism* and *Oxymoron*.

A euphemism is a figure of speech in which a vague, indirect, or mild word is substituted for a word deemed harsh, blunt, or offensive. For instance, people often say passed away rather than died because the former seems less offensive. Euphemisms abound in politics and society where politically correct words are used instead of words that seem pejorative. An oxymoron, on the other hand, is a figure of speech in which incongruous or contradictory terms are combined. For example, a deafening silence combines two contradictory concepts. For example, since there is no sound in silence, how can it be deafening?

DETERMINE THE FIGURE OF SPEECH USED IN THIS SENTENCE.

> "A yawn may be defined as a silent yell."(*G.K. Chesterton*, George Bernard Shaw, 1909)

The term "silent yell" is an oxymoron because a yell is not silent. These words do not belong together because these words are contradictory. By definition, an oxymoron combines two contradictory elements. Other examples include *real phony,* and *pretty ugly.* The expression is not a simile or personification, nor is it a hyperbole or onomatopoeia. Although it is a metaphor, the metaphor consists of an oxymoron.

DETERMINE HOW YOU CAN DISTINGUISH WHICH WORD IN THE SENTENCE IS A EUPHEMISM.

> Veronica went into the restaurant, was shown a table, and then asked the waiter where she could find a restroom.

This statement is very straight forward. It is about a woman entering a restaurant, sitting at the table, and asking where she could find a restroom. The word *restroom* is a euphemism for bathroom. It is considered less offensive to use the term *restroom* than the terms *bathroom* or *toilet.* This practice of softening our language has been in existence for many years. Euphemism means "the use of words of good omen" in Greek, and Greeks used euphemisms as substitutes for religious words such as the names of deities that were not supposed to be spoken. In addition, the practice was found in Indo-European languages as well as in Arabic languages. Today euphemisms are extremely popular and often are used to ensure political correctness of language.

VARIOUS NUANCES OF THE WORDS *BRAZEN* AND *DARING*.

Nuances are slight differences in the meanings of words that mean almost the same thing. Nuances make a word different in its tone or shade of meaning. They are similar to connotations, although usually more subtle. In the case of the words *brazen* and *daring,* while both words mean *bold, brazen* has a slightly negative aspect having to do with being shameless, forward, or overstepping. *Daring,* on the other hand, has a more positive aspect having to do with being brave or courageous. Writers often use nuance to suggest something about a character or topic without directly stating their meaning. Readers should look for nuances in language in order to understand the writer's point of view and intent.

IMPROVING COMPREHENSION

The acquisition of general academic and domain- specific words and phrases is especially important for success in academic endeavors. Without the ability to understand language at the college or career level, a student will not be prepared for the future. Students must be familiar with domain-specific words and phrases if they hope to move on in a specific field. In order to become proficient in language, a student should make lists of new words, use them in sentences, and learn to spell them. A text book's glossary is a good source for finding domain-specific words. Extended reading allows the student to improve his or her vocabulary. Again, a good reader will try to understand the meaning of a word through context. Nonetheless, if this effort fails, the student should find the precise meaning in a dictionary or glossary.

Practice Test #1

Practice Questions

1. Choose the word that correctly fills the blank in the following sentence:

Joanne still needs to finish her homework: revise her essay, _____ the next chapter, and complete the math problems.

a. reading
b. to read
c. read
d. will read

2. Our vacation time was over, but we didn't want to go home.

The bolded words represent a(n)...

a. Dependent clause
b. Independent clause
c. Relative clause
d. Adverbial clause

3. Which of the following sentences is correct?

a. I am going to buy a new car it is a blue sedan.
b. I am going to buy a new car, it is a blue sedan.
c. I am going to buy a new car; it is a blue sedan.
d. I am going to buy a new car, therefore, it is a blue sedan.

4. Which of the following sentences is correct?

a. Rachel excels in several activities, including: swimming, hiking, and biking.
b. Rachel excels in: swimming, hiking, and biking.
c. Rachel excels in several activities: swimming, hiking, and biking.
d. Rachel excels in several activities, such as: swimming, hiking, and biking.

5. Mara enjoyed great felicity when her missing dog found his way home.

What does the word "felicity" mean in this sentence?

a. Discomfort
b. Anxiety
c. Disbelief
d. Happiness

6. Choose the correct spelling of the word that completes the following sentence:

The black mangrove tree is native, or ________, to South Florida.

a. indigenous
b. endigenous
c. indegenous
d. endeginous

7. Choose the word that best fills the blank in the following sentence:

Peter is so talented with horses that the skittish colt became _______ once Peter took over his training.

a. frantic
b. docile
c. lucid
d. prudent

8. Choose the word that best fills the blank in the following sentence:

Stanley had never liked Nathan, but he grudgingly ___________ Nathan for his idea of holding a car wash for the school fundraiser.

a. exalted
b. glorified
c. honored
d. commended

9. Identify the literary device used in the following sentence:

Caroline was rendered speechless to such a degree that she talked of nothing else for the rest of the day.

a. Irony
b. Hyperbole
c. Personification
d. Euphemism

10. The detective dedicated his life to hunting down the truth.

What does "hunting down the truth" mean in this sentence?

a. The detective preferred to work with a gun.
b. The detective was determined to tell the truth.
c. The detective wanted to eradicate the truth.
d. The detective was determined to learn the truth.

Questions 11-23 refer to the following article:

Global warming and the depletion of natural resources are constant threats to the future of our planet. All people have a responsibility to be proactive participants in the fight to save Earth by working now to conserve resources for later. Participation begins with our everyday choices. From what you buy to what you do to how much you use, your decisions affect the planet and everyone around you. Now is the time to take action.

When choosing what to buy, look for **sustainable** products made from renewable or recycled resources. The packaging of the products you buy is just as important as the products themselves. Is the item minimally packaged in a recycled container? How did the product reach the store? Locally grown food and other products manufactured within your community are the best choices. The fewer miles a product traveled to reach you, the fewer resources it required.

You can continue to make a difference for the planet in how you use what you bought and the resources you have available. Remember the locally grown food you purchased? Don't pile it on your plate at dinner. Food that remains on your plate is a wasted resource, and you can always go back for seconds. You should try to be aware of your **consumption** of water and energy. Turn off the water when you brush your teeth, and limit your showers to five minutes. Turn off the lights, and don't leave appliances or chargers plugged in when not in use.

Together, we can use less, waste less, recycle more, and make the right choices. It may be the only chance we have.

11. What is the author's primary purpose in writing this article?

a. The author's purpose is to scare people.
b. The author's purpose is to warn people.
c. The author's purpose is to inspire people.
d. The author's purpose is to inform people.

12. What is the author's tone?

a. The author's tone is optimistic.
b. The author's tone is pessimistic.
c. The author's tone is matter-of-fact.
d. The author's tone is angry.

13. How does the author make a connection between the second and third paragraphs?

a. The author indicates he will now make suggestions for how to use what you bought.
b. The author indicates he will continue to give more examples of what you should buy.
c. The author indicates he will make suggestions for how to keep from buying more items.
d. The author indicates he will make suggestions for how to tell other people what to buy.

14. What is the main idea of this article?

a. People should use less water and energy.
b. People should make responsible choices in what they purchase and how they use their available resources.
c. People are quickly destroying the earth, and there is no way to stop the destruction.
d. People should organize everyone they know to join the fight to save the environment.

15. Which organizational pattern did the author use?

a. Comparison and contrast
b. Chronological order
c. Cause and effect
d. Problem/solution

16. Why does the author say it is important to buy locally grown food?

a. Buying locally grown food supports people in your community.
b. Locally grown food travels the least distance to reach you, and therefore uses fewer resources.
c. Locally grown food uses less packaging.
d. Locally grown food is healthier for you because it has been exposed to fewer pesticides.

17. Which of the following suggestions does the author give for conserving resources?

a. Turn off the water when you brush your teeth.
b. Use a ceiling fan instead of an air conditioner.
c. Drive an electric car instead of a gas-powered car.
d. Use energy-saving appliances.

18. What does the author say is the place to begin saving our planet?

a. The place to begin is with getting rid of products that are not earth friendly.
b. The place to begin is with using less water when we take a shower.
c. The place to begin is with the choices we make every day.
d. The place to begin is with buying locally-grown food.

19. What does the author imply will happen if people do not follow his suggestions?

a. The author implies we will run out of resources in the next 10 years.
b. The author implies water and energy prices will rise sharply in the near future.
c. The author implies global warming and the depletion of natural resources will continue.
d. The author implies local farmers will lose their farms.

20. You are working with a group to compile further research on what people can do to help the environment. Your teacher has asked your group to present a broad overview of the topic. Which of the following would be the best choice for dividing the topic among the individuals in your group?

a. Products that can be recycled, products that cannot be recycled, and products that should not be recycled.
b. Products that can be recycled, products that consume less energy, and products that use recycled packaging.
c. Products that can be recycled, hybrid cars, and water conservation.
d. Products that can be recycled, products that consume less energy, and accomplishing everyday tasks using environmentally friendly practices.

21. "When choosing what to buy, look for sustainable products made from renewable or recycled resources."

What does the word "sustainable" mean in the context of this selection?

a. Able to be maintained or kept in existence
b. Produced locally
c. Chosen for specific characteristics
d. Manufactured using an energy efficient process

22. "You should try to be aware of your consumption of water and energy."

What does the word "consumption" mean in the context of this selection?

a. Using the greatest amount
b. Illness of the lungs
c. Using the least amount
d. Depletion of goods

23. The author makes a general suggestion to the reader: "You should try to be aware of your consumption of water and energy." Which of the following is one way the author specifies that this suggestion be carried out?

a. Food that remains on your plate is a wasted resource, and you can always go back for a second helping.
b. Locally grown food and other products manufactured within your community are the best choices.
c. Turn off the lights, and don't leave appliances or chargers plugged in when not in use.
d. Participation begins with our everyday choices.

Question 24 refers to the following excerpt from George Washington's Farewell Address:

> "Towards the preservation of your government and the permanency of your present happy state, it is not only requisite that you steadily discountenance irregular oppositions to its authority, but that you should be upon your guard against the spirit of innovation upon its principles, however specious the pretexts. One method of assault may be to effect alterations in the forms of the Constitution tending to impair the energy of the system, and so to undermine what cannot be directly overthrown. In all the changes to which you may be invited, remember that time and habit are as necessary to fix the true character of governments as of any other human institutions; that experience is the surest standard by which the real tendency of existing constitutions of government can be tried; that changes upon the credit of mere hypothesis and opinion expose you to perpetual change from the successive and endless variety of hypothesis and opinion. And remember also, that for the efficacious management of your common interests, in a country so extensive as ours, a government of as much force and strength as is consistent with the perfect security of liberty is indispensable. Liberty itself will find in such a government, with powers properly distributed and arranged, its surest guardian and protector. In my opinion, the real danger in our system is, that the general government, organized as at present, will prove too weak rather than too powerful."

24. Which of the following provides the best summary of President Washington's advice in this selection?

a. President Washington advises the people of the United States to give the existing government a chance to work before deciding that any amendments need to be made.
b. President Washington advises the people of the United States to make as many alterations to the Constitution as they deem necessary to preserve liberty.
c. President Washington advises the people of the United States to recognize that the existing government is too weak to properly manage such a large and powerful nation.
d. President Washington advises the people of the United States to continue to fight for liberty and justice for all.

Questions 25-34 refer to the following selection from Pride and Prejudice by Jane Austen:

It is a truth universally acknowledged, that a single man in possession of a good fortune, must be in want of a wife.

> However little known the feelings or views of such a man may be on his first entering a neighbourhood, this truth is so well fixed in the minds of the surrounding families, that he is considered the rightful property of some one or other of their daughters.

"My dear Mr. Bennet," said his lady to him one day, "have you heard that Netherfield Park is let at last?"

Mr. Bennet replied that he had not.

"But it is," returned she; "for Mrs. Long has just been here, and she told me all about it."

Mr. Bennet made no answer.

"Do you not want to know who has taken it?" cried his wife impatiently.

"You want to tell me, and I have no objection to hearing it."

This was invitation enough.

"Why, my dear, you must know, Mrs. Long says that Netherfield is taken by a young man of large fortune from the north of England; that he came down on Monday in a chaise and four to see the place, and was so much delighted with it, that he agreed with Mr. Morris immediately; that he is to take possession before Michaelmas, and some of his servants are to be in the house by the end of next week."

"What is his name?"

"Bingley."

"Is he married or single?"

"Oh! Single, my dear, to be sure! A single man of large fortune; four or five thousand a year. What a fine thing for our girls!"

"How so? How can it affect them?"

"My dear Mr. Bennet," replied his wife, "how can you be so tiresome! You must know that I am thinking of his marrying one of them."

"Is that his design in settling here?"

"Design! Nonsense, how can you talk so! But it is very likely that he may fall in love with one of them, and therefore you must visit him as soon as he comes."

"I see no occasion for that. You and the girls may go, or you may send them by themselves, which perhaps will be still better, for as you are as handsome as any of them, Mr. Bingley may like you the best of the party."

25. What is the central idea of this selection?

a. A new neighbor is due to arrive who may become good friends with Mr. and Mrs. Bennet.
b. A new neighbor is due to arrive who may be a prospective husband for one of the Bennet daughters.
c. A new neighbor is due to arrive who may be a good business connection for Mr. Bennet.
d. A new neighbor is due to arrive who has already expressed an interest in marrying one of the Bennet daughters.

26. How does Mrs. Bennet feel about the arrival of Mr. Bingley?

a. Mrs. Bennet is excited about the arrival of Mr. Bingley.
b. Mrs. Bennet is nervous about the arrival of Mr. Bingley.
c. Mrs. Bennet is afraid the arrival of Mr. Bingley will upset Mr. Bennet.
d. Mrs. Bennet is indifferent to the arrival of Mr. Bingley.

27. What does Mrs. Bennet expect from Mr. Bennet?

a. Mrs. Bennet expects Mr. Bennet to invite Mr. Bingley to a dinner party.
b. Mrs. Bennet expects Mr. Bennet to offer one of his daughters in marriage to Mr. Bingley.
c. Mrs. Bennet expects Mr. Bennet to pay a visit to Mr. Bingley.
d. Mrs. Bennet expects Mr. Bennet to invite Mr. Bingley to a ball in his honor.

28. What does Mrs. Bennet expect from Mr. Bingley?

a. Mrs. Bennet expects Mr. Bingley to be interested in marrying one of her daughters.
b. Mrs. Bennet expects Mr. Bingley to be interested in receiving a visit from Mr. Bennet.
c. Mrs. Bennet expects Mr. Bingley to love living at Netherfield Park.
d. Mrs. Bennet expects Mr. Bingley to ask for her help in choosing a wife for himself.

29. Which of the following statements best describes Mrs. Bennet's feelings about her husband as indicated by this selection?

a. Mrs. Bennet is tired of her husband.
b. Mrs. Bennet is exasperated by her husband.
c. Mrs. Bennet is afraid of her husband.
d. Mrs. Bennet is indifferent toward her husband.

30. Which of the following statements best describes Mr. Bennet's feelings about his wife as indicated by this selection?

a. Mr. Bennet thinks his wife is a great beauty.
b. Mr. Bennet thinks his wife is a wonderful mother.
c. Mr. Bennet thinks his wife is intolerable.
d. Mr. Bennet thinks his wife is silly.

31. This selection is set in England at the beginning of the 19th century. Drawing on information from this selection, what could you conclude was a primary goal for young women in England during this time period?

a. To marry
b. To marry a man with money
c. To entertain the neighbors
d. To be courted by as many men as possible

32. "It is a truth universally acknowledged, that a single man in possession of a good fortune, must be in want of a wife."

Which of the following most nearly matches the meaning of the bolded phrase?

a. Everyone knows
b. The universe has decided
c. It is a documented fact
d. It is best to tell the truth

33. "It is a truth universally acknowledged, that a single man in possession of a good fortune, must be in want of a wife."

Which of the following most nearly matches the meaning of the bolded phrase?

a. An unmarried man always wants to get married.
b. An unmarried man must want to give his money away.
c. An unmarried man with money always wants to get married.
d. An unmarried man can increase his fortune by getting married.

34. "Is that his design in settling here?"

What does the word design mean in the context of this selection?

a. Intention
b. Drawing
c. Creation
d. Improvisation

For questions 35-40, choose the best sentences to create a paragraph IN SUPPORT of boarding schools as an educational alternative. The paragraph should make an argument in favor of boarding schools while ACKNOWLEDGING anticipated criticisms.

35. Choose the best sentence:

a. Boarding schools are a great alternative to day schools, allowing students to have independence, develop friendships, and make the most of school facilities.
b. Boarding schools are a good choice for some people, but not a good choice for others.
c. Boarding schools are a great choice for students who live in other countries.
d. Boarding schools are not a good alternative to day schools because they restrict students' social circles and time with families.

36. Choose the best sentence:

a. Boarding school students grow up too quickly because they lack the supervision that students usually receive when they live at home. This can lead to problems later on.
b. Traveling abroad during the summer gives students an opportunity to expand their horizons and learn about the world.
c. Boarding school students are afforded an opportunity to develop their independence in a safe and controlled setting. This can lead to an increased sense of responsibility that will serve these students well in college and beyond.
d. Students often perform poorly their first year in a boarding school. It can be difficult to transition from a home situation where parents help monitor academic progress to a school situation where students are fully responsible for their own work.

37. Choose the best sentence:

a. The anxieties of social situations often experienced during the teenage years are eased by the close familiarity boarding school students share with their peers.
b. The problem with boarding schools is that students have less time to spend with their families. Students do, however, have a great opportunity to develop friendships with peers.
c. Students who attend boarding schools live in an environment that fosters friendships with both their peers and their teachers. The bonds created during the school years can continue as lifelong friendships.
d. Although students who attend boarding schools spend less time with their families, they often develop lifelong friendships with their peers. There is a unique sense of community and cooperation in a school where the students and staff live and work together.

38. Choose the best sentence:

a. Critics argue that a boarding school community represents a limited social circle; however, most boarding schools draw their student population from a wide geographical area, which creates a more diverse grouping than the population of a local day school.
b. Boarding school students are limited to socializing with their classmates and teachers.
c. Students from all over the world attend boarding schools.
d. Boarding schools would be improved by offering students opportunities for internships that take them out of the school and into the community.

39. Choose the best sentence:

a. Some boarding schools offer specialized curriculums that allow students to focus on a subject of choice.
b. Both boarding and day schools often have useful facilities such as libraries, computer labs, and gymnasiums. The opportunity to take advantage of these facilities is greater in a boarding school where the location is convenient to students and the hours are flexible.
c. Boarding schools always have more money than day schools.
d. Some day schools offer extracurricular activities for students who wish to participate in sports, music, or drama.

40. Choose the best sentence:

a. Boarding schools usually require their students to wear uniforms.
b. Boarding and day schools offer students wonderful educational and extracurricular opportunities.
c. Boarding school is the right choice for many students.
d. Boarding school is the right choice for many students, bringing them a chance for independence, lifelong friendships, access to beneficial facilities, and memories that will last a lifetime.

41. Choose the sentence that most effectively follows the conventions of Standard Written English:

a. Theodor Seuss Geisel published his first children's book in 1937 under the pseudonym Dr. Seuss.
b. It wasn't until 1937 that Theodor Seuss Geisel first published a children's book with the pseudonym Dr. Seuss on it.
c. The pseudonym Dr. Seuss was used to publish Theodor Seuss Geisel's first children's book which happened in 1937.
d. In 1937, Dr. Seuss was the pseudonym used by Theodor Seuss Geisel when he published his first children's book.

42. Choose the sentence that most effectively follows the conventions of Standard Written English:

a. The light bulb and the phonograph are the best known inventions of the inventor Thomas Edison who also invented many other things.
b. Thomas Edison was a prolific inventor best known for inventing the light bulb and the phonograph.
c. Thomas Edison invented prolifically including the light bulb, the phonograph, and many other inventions.
d. The many inventions of Thomas Edison include the light bulb and the phonograph, probably the best known of all of them.

Directions for questions 43-45: Read the following sentences and choose the underlined word or phrase that should be changed so that the sentence follows the conventions of Standard Written English. For sentences that are correct as written, choose option D.

43. <u>John conducted</u> the interview with wit and <u>verve, posing</u> question after question to Nancy <u>and I</u>.

a. John conducted
b. verve, posing
c. and I
d. No error

44. Each student <u>must choose</u> <u>their topic</u> and submit a <u>preliminary outline</u> before Friday.

a. must choose
b. their topic
c. preliminary outline
d. No error

45. It <u>was time</u> to go <u>home, but</u> we planned <u>to return to</u> the mountains again next summer.

a. was time
b. home, but
c. to return to
d. No error

46. Choose the words that best fill the blanks in the following sentence:

King George III was ________ to have the American colonists ________ taxes to Britain on items such as tea and paper.

a. devious, remand
b. prudent, attribute
c. detrimental, tribute
d. determined, pay

47. Choose the words that best fill the blanks in the following sentence:

Susan B. Anthony was ________ that women were ________ the same rights as men, such as equal pay and the right to vote.

a. glad, written
b. outraged, denied
c. determined, have
d. credulous, given

Questions 48-51 refer to the following paragraph:

> Margaritte stood nervously in the wings of the stage, waiting for her cue. The music from the orchestra swelled around her. She could almost see the colors and shapes it made in the air. With one foot, Margaritte kept time with the beat. Any minute now, it would be her turn. The note sounded, and Margaritte flew from the wings.

48. Which of the following would be the best introductory sentence for this paragraph?

a. Margaritte wore her favorite pink tutu.
b. Margaritte looked at the other dancers waiting with her backstage.
c. Margaritte had been taking dance lessons since she was nine years old.
d. Margaritte was about to begin the most important performance of her dancing career.

49. Which of the following would be the best sentence to add sensory detail to this paragraph?

a. The people in the audience looked like a garden in their colorful attire.
b. The stage was draped in black so that the dancers' costumes stood out.
c. The sound of the music reverberated in Margaritte's chest, becoming a part of her.
d. Margaritte's tights felt itchy against her legs.

50. Which of the following would be the best sentence to add descriptive detail to this paragraph?

a. The music formed the shapes of birds that soared above the stage and disappeared over the audience.
b. This was Margaritte's favorite music to dance to.
c. Tapping her toe to the beat of the music, Margaritte found herself growing increasingly nervous.
d. Margaritte felt the audience would see her nervousness as soon as she stepped onto the stage.

51. Which of the following would be the best concluding sentence for this paragraph?

a. Margaritte danced onto the stage as the music swirled around her.
b. Margaritte danced onto the stage; her moment had finally come.
c. When the dance recital was over, Margaritte was tired.
d. The other dancers moved onto the stage with Margaritte.

Questions 52-54 refer to the following paragraph:

Many fears about snakes arise from misconceptions. People are often afraid that all snakes are venomous creatures looking for people to bite. However, of the approximately 2400 species of snakes, only 270 are venomous. Venomous snakes have fangs, hollow teeth with tiny holes at the bottom through which venom is released. Although venomous snakes should be treated carefully, there is no need to fear that a snake will bite you without provocation. Like many other animals, snakes will only attack when they feel threatened.

52. Which of the following would be the best introductory sentence for this paragraph?

a. Many people think snakes have slimy skin, but they do not.
b. Gaining knowledge about snakes is the best way to learn to live harmoniously with these misunderstood reptiles.
c. A rattlesnake will sound its rattle to warn people not to come near.
d. Snakes shed their skin when it gets too small.

53. Which of the following sentences is not essential to explain the primary premise of the paragraph?

a. People are often afraid that all snakes are venomous creatures looking for people to bite.
b. However, of the approximately 2400 species of snakes, only 270 are venomous.
c. Venomous snakes have fangs, hollow teeth with tiny holes at the bottom through which venom is released.
d. Although venomous snakes should be treated carefully, there is no need to fear that a snake will bite you without provocation.

54. Which of the following would be the best concluding sentence for this paragraph?

a. There is no need to be fearful of snakes as long as you are careful.
b. People in the desert are the only ones who should be afraid of snakes.
c. You should learn the names of each species of snake.
d. Snakes are more afraid of people than people are of them.

Answers and Explanations

ELA-Literacy.L.9-10.1a

1. C: "Read" (present tense form of the verb) maintains the parallel structure of the sentence and matches the verb tense for "revise" and "complete." The other answer choices represent the present participle ("reading"), infinitive ("to read"), and future tense ("will read") of the word.

ELA-Literacy.L.9-10.1b

2. B: The highlighted words represent an independent clause because they contain both a subject and verb and because they express a complete thought.

ELA-Literacy.L.9-10.2a

3. C: "I am going to buy a new car" and "it is a blue sedan" are independent clauses (they each contain a subject and a verb and express a complete thought). It is appropriate to join two independent clauses in a single sentence with a semicolon. Choice A is a run-on sentence. Choice B is a comma splice. Choice D uses a comma to precede the conjunctive adverb "therefore," which is incorrect.

ELA-Literacy.L.9-10.2b

4. C: It is appropriate to use a colon to introduce a list. It is not appropriate to use a colon following a preposition (choice B) or after the phrases "including" and "such as," which make the use of a colon redundant (choices A and D).

ELA-Literacy.L.9-10.4a

5. D: The context of the sentence indicates that Mara would feel great happiness.

ELA-Literacy.L.9-10.2c

6. A: The correct spelling of the word is "indigenous."

ELA-Literacy.L.9-10.6

7. B: The word "docile" means easily taught or ready to be taught. The sentence should read: Peter is so talented with horses that the skittish colt became docile once Peter took over his training.

ELA-Literacy.L.9-10.5b

8. D: Although the word choices all have similar denotations, the context of the sentence, and especially the use of the word "grudgingly," indicate that Stanley gave only a perfunctory congratulations to Nathan for his good idea.

ELA-Literacy.L.9-10.5a

9. A: Irony is an expression where words are attributed with the opposite of their usual meaning. The fact that Caroline was not rendered speechless, but quite the opposite, is indicated by the fact that she did not stop talking the rest of the day.

ELA-Literacy.L.9-10.5a

10. D: "Hunting down the truth" is a figure of speech that means "determined to learn the truth." This is indicated by the context of the sentence which references the life goal of a detective.

ELA-Literacy.RI.9-10.6

11. D: Various parts of the article are intended to scare (choice A), warn (choice B), and inspire (choice C) people, but the primary purpose of the article is to offer practical advice about what products people should buy and how to use their available resources to make responsible decisions for the future of our planet.

ELA-Literacy.RI.9-10.6

12. C: The author does not make predictions of a radically rejuvenated planet (choice A) or the complete annihilation of life as we know it (choice B). The author is also not accusatory in his descriptions (choice D). Instead, the author states what he believes to be the current state of the planet's environment, and makes practical suggestions for making better use of its resources in the future.

ELA-Literacy.RI.9-10.3

13. A: The author begins the third paragraph with, "You can continue to make a difference for the planet in how you use what you bought and the resources you have available." This sentence makes the connection between the second paragraph which deals with what people should buy and the third paragraph which makes suggestions for how to use what they have.

ELA-Literacy.RI.9-10.2

14. B: The author does suggest that people should use less water and energy (choice A), but these are only two suggestions among many and not the main idea of the article. The article does not say that people are destroying the earth (choice C) or make a suggestion that people organize their acquaintances (choice D).

ELA-Literacy.RI.9-10.3

15. D: The author presents the problems of global warming and the rapid depletion of the planet's natural resources and offers several practical suggestions for how to stop global warming and use remaining resources judiciously.

ELA-Literacy.RI.9-10.1

16. B: As the passage states: "Locally grown food and other products manufactured within your community are the best choices. The fewer miles a product traveled to reach you, the fewer resources it required."

ELA-Literacy.RI.9-10.1

17. A: Although the other answer choices do represent ways to conserve resources, choice A is the only suggestion the author makes within this article.

ELA-Literacy.RI.9-10.1

18. C: The author makes suggestions to use less water (choice B) and buy locally grown food (choice D), but they are not suggested as the place to begin saving the planet. The author does not suggest getting rid of products that are not earth friendly (choice A). The author states: "Participation begins with our everyday choices."

ELA-Literacy.SL.9-10.1a

19. C: The author does not mention running out of resources in a specific time period (choice A), the cost of water and energy (choice B), or the possibility of hardship for local farmers (choice D).

ELA-Literacy.SL.9-10.1b

20. D: Choice D gives the broadest interpretation of the topic. Choice A focuses solely on recycling; choice B focuses on the choice of products to be purchased; and choice C focuses on recycling, one type of energy-saving product (hybrid cars), and ways to conserve one resource (water).

ELA-Literacy.RI.9-10.4

21. A: "When choosing what to buy, look for sustainable products made from renewable or recycled resources." The context of this sentence indicates that sustainable means renewable or able to be used again.

ELA-Literacy.RI.9-10.4

22. D: As the passage states: "You should try to be aware of your consumption of water and energy. Turn off the water when you brush your teeth, and limit your showers to five minutes. Turn off the lights, and don't leave appliances or chargers plugged in when not in use." The contexts of these sentences indicate that consumption means the depletion of goods (e.g., water and energy).

ELA-Literacy.RI.9-10.5

23. C: Of the choices available, this is the only sentence that offers specific ideas for carrying out the author's suggestion to the reader of limiting consumption of energy.

ELA-Literacy.RI.9-10.9

24. A: Washington urges people to "remember that time and habit are as necessary to fix the true character of governments as of any other human institutions; that experience is the surest standard by which the real tendency of existing constitutions of government can be tried."

ELA-Literacy.RL.9-10.2

25. B: There is no indication in the passage that the Bennets are interested in becoming friends with Mr. Bingley (choice A), that Mr. Bingley would be a valuable business connection (choice C), or that Mr. Bingley has any prior knowledge of the Bennet daughters (choice D). Mrs. Bennet tells her husband that a new neighbor is moving in: "Mrs. Long says that Netherfield is taken by a young man of large fortune." Mrs. Bennet is sure he will make an excellent husband for one of her daughters: "You must know that I am thinking of his marrying one of them."

ELA-Literacy.RL.9-10.1

26. A: Mrs. Bennet feels that Mr. Bingley is likely to marry one of her daughters. She tells her husband that Mr. Bingley is a "single man of large fortune; four or five thousand a year. What a fine thing for our girls!"

ELA-Literacy.RL.9-10.1

27. C: Mrs. Bennet wants her husband to be acquainted with Mr. Bingley so that he can introduce Mr. Bingley to their daughters: "But it is very likely that he may fall in love with one of them, and therefore you must visit him as soon as he comes."

ELA-Literacy.RL.9-10.1

28. A: Mrs. Bennet remarks to her husband, "But it is very likely that he may fall in love with one of them, and therefore you must visit him as soon as he comes."

ELA-Literacy.RL.9-10.3

29. B: Mrs. Bennet is exasperated by her husband, meaning that she is frustrated or annoyed and fed up with her husband's seeming indifference to Mr. Bingley: "'My dear Mr. Bennet,' replied his wife, 'how can you be so tiresome!'" Being annoyed would indicate that she is not indifferent toward him. She also is the person who initiated the dialog and seems to eagerly want to talk to him about her ideas. This would indicate that she is neither tired nor afraid of her husband.

ELA-Literacy.RL.9-10.3

30. D: Mr. Bennet baits his wife throughout the dialogue: "You want to tell me, and I have no objection to hearing it." Upon hearing about the arrival of Mr. Bingley, he pretends that he doesn't know his wife is looking upon Mr. Bingley as a potential son-in-law: "How so? How can it affect them?" He even asks if Mr. Bingley has the same aim as Mrs. Bennet: "Is that his design in settling here?"

ELA-Literacy.RL.9-10.6

31. B: The evidence in this selection indicates that marrying a man with money was a primary goal for young women. Mrs. Bennet tells Mr. Bennet that Mr. Bingley is "A single man of large fortune; four or five thousand a year." Mrs. Bennet further indicates that she is thrilled with the news because of Mr. Bingley's potential as a husband for one of her daughters: "What a fine thing for our girls... You must know that I am thinking of his marrying one of them."

ELA-Literacy.RL.9-10.4

32. A: "It is a truth universally acknowledged" means that something is understood to be true by the general public.

ELA-Literacy.RL.9-10.4

33. C: "A single man in possession of a good fortune, must be in want of a wife" means that if a man has enough money to support a wife in comfort, he must want to find a wife as soon as possible.

ELA-Literacy.RL.9-10.4

34. A: Mr. Bennet is facetiously asking if the idea of marriage (particularly to one of his own daughters) was Mr. Bingley's intention when he agreed to rent Netherfield Park.

ELA-Literacy.W.9-10.1a

35. A: This is the only answer choice that is clearly in support of boarding schools as an educational alternative.

ELA-Literacy.SL.9-10.4

36. C: Choices A and D are not in support of boarding schools. Choice B is off topic.

ELA-Literacy.W.9-10.1c

37. D: This is the only answer choice that both acknowledges a criticism of boarding schools (less time with family) and points out the corresponding benefit (peer and teacher relationships).

ELA-Literacy.W.9-10.1b

38. A: This is the only answer choice that both acknowledges a criticism of boarding schools (limited social circle) and points out the corresponding benefit (diverse population).

ELA-Literacy.S.9-10.6

39. B: This is the only answer choice that makes a clear argument in favor of boarding schools.

ELA-Literacy.W.9-10.1e

40. D: This is the only answer choice that provides a summary of the benefits of boarding schools.

ELA-Literacy.W.9-10.4

41. A: This sentence best conveys the information without using too many words (choice C) or having an awkward construction (choices B and D).

ELA-Literacy.W.9-10.4

42. B: This sentence best conveys the information without using too many words (choices A and D) or having an awkward construction (choice C).

ELA-Literacy.W.9-10.5

43. C: The sentence should read: John conducted the interview with wit and verve, posing question after question to Nancy and me.

ELA-Literacy.W.9-10.5

44. B: The sentence should read: Each student must choose his or her topic and submit a preliminary outline before Friday.

ELA-Literacy.W.9-10.5

45. D: The sentence is correct as written.

ELA-Literacy.W.9-10.4

46. D: The sentence should read: King George III was determined to have the American colonists pay taxes to Britain on items such as tea and paper.

ELA-Literacy.W.9-10.4

47. B: The sentence should read: Susan B. Anthony was outraged that women were denied the same rights as men, such as equal pay and the right to vote.

ELA-Literacy.W.9-10.3a

48. D: Choices A and C are detail sentences that do not convey the setting or event of the rest of the paragraph. Choice B references other dancers not mentioned anywhere else in the paragraph.

ELA-Literacy. W.9-10.3d

49. C: This is the only choice that expands on Margaritte's feelings about the music and echoes the tension of the event. Choices A and B refer to people (the audience, the other dancers) outside of Margaritte and her experience with the music as she waits for her cue, which is not the point of the passage. Choice D talks about Margaritte's clothing, which is not mentioned anywhere else in the paragraph.

ELA-Literacy.W.9-10.3b

50. A: Choices B, C, and D are details, but do not invoke a particular image.

ELA-Literacy.W.9-10.3e

51. B: This sentence tells what is happening at the moment and reflects on the tension that is apparent throughout the rest of the paragraph. Choice A only tells what is happening at the moment. Choice C refers to a time beyond the time referenced in the paragraph. Choice D introduces other dancers not mentioned previously in the paragraph.

ELA-Literacy.W.9-10.2a

52. B: The other choices are detail sentences and do not express the main idea of the paragraph.

ELA-Literacy.W.9-10.2b

53. C: Of the choices given, this sentence does not add anything to the paragraph's central premise that people should educate themselves about snakes instead of believing that snakes are looking for someone to attack.

ELA-Literacy.W.9-10.2f

54. A: This is the only choice that sums up the tone and purpose of the paragraph.

Practice Test #2

Practice Questions

1. Which of the following sentences is correct?

a. Sonja works very hard, she is tired all the time.
b. Sonja works very hard she is tired all the time.
c. Sonja works very hard, however, she is tired all the time.
d. Sonja works very hard; she is tired all the time.

2. Although Scott is fond of pudding, he chose chocolate cake for his dessert.

The bolded words represent a(n)...

a. Dependent clause
b. Independent clause
c. Relative clause
d. Adverbial clause

3. Choose the word that correctly fills the blank in the following sentence:

Mrs. Simmons asked her students to get their books, read the first chapter, and _____ the questions at the end.

a. answer
b. to answer
c. answering
d. will answer

4. Choose the correct spelling of the word that fills the blank in the following sentence:

Plastic trash that ends up in the ocean can have a _________, or harmful, effect on marine life.

a. diliterious
b. deleterious
c. delaterious
d. dilaterious

5. Which of the following sentences is correct?

a. Jason loves candy including: lollipops, chocolate bars, and gumdrops.
b. Jason loves candy except: lollipops, chocolate bars, and gumdrops.
c. Jason loves candy, for example: lollipops, chocolate bars, and gumdrops.
d. Jason loves candy: lollipops, chocolate bars, and gumdrops.

6. What does the word cursory mean in this sentence?

The immigration officer gave Maria's passport a cursory examination before quickly moving on to the next person in line.

a. Lazy
b. Angry
c. Hasty
d. Careful

7. Choose the word set that best fills the blanks in the following sentence:

As a student council ________, Travis endeavored to ________ his peers to the best of his ability.

a. represent, representational
b. representative, represent
c. representation, represent
d. represent, representative

8. Identify the literary device used in the following sentence:

It was time to go home; the trees waved a fond farewell to speed us on our way.

a. Irony
b. Hyperbole
c. Personification
d. Euphemism

9. Choose the word that best fills the blank in the following sentence:

The selection of the winning lottery numbers is entirely __________ with numbers being drawn at random out of a large ball.

a. diverse
b. arbitrary
c. deliberate
d. ubiquitous

10. What does let the cat out of the bag mean in this sentence?

We'd planned to surprise Margaret with a party for her sixteenth birthday, but the surprise was ruined when Theresa let the cat out of the bag.

a. Disclosed a secret
b. Released a cat from confinement
c. Opposed having a party
d. Declined to participate

Questions 11-24 refer to the following passage:

Helen Keller was born on June 27, 1880. She was a happy and healthy child until the age of 19 months when she fell ill with a terrible fever. Although Helen recovered from the fever, it left her both deaf and blind.

Helen was loved and cared for by her doting parents, but her behavior became erratic after she lost her hearing and sight, with unpredictable outbursts of temper. Her parents were at a loss how to reach her and teach her how to behave. Helen herself was frustrated and lonely in her dark, silent world. All of that began to change in March 1887 when Anne Sullivan came to live with the Kellers and be Helen's teacher.

Anne taught Helen to communicate by forming letters with her fingers held in another person's hand. In this way, Teacher, as Helen called her, taught her pupil to spell cake, doll, and milk. However, it was not until Anne spelled w-a-t-e-r in Helen's hands as cold water gushed over both of them that Helen made the exciting connection between the words and the world around her. This connection engendered an insatiable curiosity within Helen. After that day, Helen learned at an incredible rate with Teacher by her side.

Helen went on to graduate from Radcliffe College. She became a famous writer, speaker, and advocate. The story of Helen's remarkable life is known worldwide. Anne Sullivan and Helen Keller were inseparable until Anne's death in 1936. Teacher shined a light in Helen's dark world and showed her the way.

11. Which organizational pattern does the author use?

a. Comparison and contrast
b. Chronological order
c. Cause and effect
d. Problem/solution

12. Which of the following would make the best topic sentence for this passage?

a. Helen Keller, with the untiring help of her teacher Anne Sullivan, became a shining example of how to rise above disabilities.
b. Anne Sullivan helped Helen Keller break free from the dark silence inflicted by a childhood fever.
c. Helen Keller and Anne Sullivan were the greatest of friends.
d. Helen Keller was a brave woman who overcame many obstacles on her road to success.

13. What is the author's primary purpose in writing this passage?

a. To inform people about Helen Keller's college career
b. To inform people about Anne Sullivan's life
c. To inform people about services available for the deaf and blind
d. To inform people about Helen Keller's life

14. How does the author make a connection between the second and third paragraphs?

a. The author begins the third paragraph by continuing to talk about Helen's parents who were introduced in the second paragraph.
b. The author organizes the second and third paragraphs the same way.
c. The author ends the second paragraph with the advent of Anne Sullivan in Helen's life, and begins the third paragraph with the most important contribution Anne made to Helen's education.
d. The author uses the third paragraph to elaborate on Helen's frustration and resulting temper tantrums introduced in the second paragraph.

15. What is the author's tone in this passage?

a. Indifferent
b. Censorious
c. Admiring
d. Impartial

16. Why was Helen frustrated as a child?

a. Helen was frustrated that her parents could not teach her to communicate.
b. Helen was frustrated that she couldn't communicate with other people.
c. Helen was frustrated that Anne came to live with the Kellers.
d. Helen was frustrated that she was unable to make the connection between the words cake, doll, and milk and the objects they represent.

17. What was the turning point in Helen's life?

a. When Helen learned to connect feeling water on her hands with the word "water."
b. When Helen graduated from Radcliffe College.
c. When Helen contracted the fever that took away her hearing and sight.
d. When Anne Sullivan came to live with the Kellers and be Helen's teacher.

18. Which of the following can you infer was true about Helen's parents?

a. Helen's parents were frustrated that they were unable to help Helen communicate.
b. Helen's parents were jealous that Anne Sullivan was closer to Helen than they were.
c. Helen's parents were glad to give Anne Sullivan full responsibility for Helen.
d. Helen's parents wanted their daughter to graduate from Radcliffe College.

19. What does the word "engendered" mean as it is used in this sentence?
This connection engendered an insatiable curiosity within Helen.

a. Caused to exist
b. Made sense of
c. Connected
d. Satisfied

20. What does the word "insatiable" mean as it is used in this sentence?
This connection engendered an insatiable curiosity within Helen.

a. Unbelievable
b. Indestructible
c. Unsatisfiable
d. Indescribable

Questions 21-25 refer to the following passage:

In the United States, the foreign language requirement for high school graduation is decided at the state level. This means the requirement varies, with some states deciding to forego a foreign language requirement altogether (www.ncssfl.org). It is necessary that these states reconsider their position and amend their requirements to reflect compulsory completion of a course of one or more foreign languages. Studying a foreign language has become increasingly important for the global economy. As technology continues to make international business relations increasingly easy, people need to keep up by increasing their communication capabilities. High school graduates with foreign language credits have been shown to have an increased college acceptance rate. In addition, students who have mastered more than one language typically find themselves in greater demand when they reach the job market. Students who did not study a foreign language often find themselves unable to obtain a job at all.

21. What is the main idea of this passage?

a. Studying a foreign language will help graduating students find jobs after high school.
b. Studying a foreign language should be a mandatory requirement for high school graduation.
c. Studying a foreign language helps students gain an understanding of other cultures.
d. Studying a foreign language is essential if a student hopes to get into college.

22. Which of the following statements represents the best summary of the claims made in this passage?

a. Studying a foreign language is important if you want to graduate from high school and get a job.
b. Studying a foreign language is important for the global economy because of the technological advances that have been made in international communications.
c. Studying a foreign language is important for the global economy, college acceptance rates, and becoming a sought-after candidate in the job market.
d. Studying a foreign language is important for college acceptance rates and obtaining a job after college.

23. Which of the following statements represents an EXAGGERATED claim in support of the argument presented in this passage?

a. In the United States, the foreign language requirement for high school graduation is decided at the state level.
b. Studying a foreign language has become increasingly important for the global economy.
c. High school graduates with foreign language credits have been shown to have an increased college acceptance rate.
d. Students who did not study a foreign language often find themselves unable to obtain a job at all.

24. Which of the following would be a useful source of information to determine the validity of the argument presented in this passage?

a. A survey of high school students' preferences with regard to foreign language requirements
b. A comparison of the correlation between a second language introduced at home and subsequent college acceptance rates
c. A survey that asks parents to select the foreign language they would like their children to study in high school
d. A comparison of the correlation between high school students' study of a foreign language and subsequent college acceptance rates

25. Which of the following would be the best concluding statement for this passage?

a. States should consider how important foreign languages are for the global economy when making their policies regarding foreign language requirements for graduation from high school.
b. Policies regarding a foreign language requirement for graduation from high school should take into account the importance of foreign languages for the global economy and the correlation between foreign languages and increased college acceptance rates and employment opportunities.
c. High school graduation requirements should include a foreign language class because of the influence knowledge of a second language has on college acceptance rates.
d. Policies regarding a foreign language requirement for graduation from high school should take into account how difficult it is to obtain a job in today's economy for those who do not have knowledge of more than one language.

Questions 26-35 refer to the following selection from Little Women by Louisa May Alcott:

"Christmas won't be Christmas without any presents," grumbled Jo, lying on the rug.

"It's so dreadful to be poor!" sighed Meg, looking down at her old dress.

"I don't think it's fair for some girls to have plenty of pretty things, and other girls nothing at all," added little Amy, with an injured sniff.

"We've got Father and Mother, and each other," said Beth contentedly from her corner.

The four young faces on which the firelight shone brightened at the cheerful words, but darkened again as Jo said sadly, "We haven't got Father, and shall not have him for a long time." She didn't say "perhaps never," but each silently added it, thinking of Father far away, where the fighting was.

Nobody spoke for a minute; then Meg said in an altered tone, "You know the reason Mother proposed not having any presents this Christmas was because it is going to be a hard winter for everyone; and she thinks we ought not to spend money for pleasure, when our men are suffering so in the army. We can't do much, but we can make our little sacrifices, and ought to do it gladly. But I am afraid I don't," and Meg shook her head, as she thought regretfully of all the pretty things she wanted.

"But I don't think the little we should spend would do any good. We've each got a dollar, and the army wouldn't be much helped by our giving that. I agree not to expect anything from Mother or you, but I do want to buy Undine and Sintran for myself. I've wanted it so long," said Jo, who was a bookworm.

"I planned to spend mine in new music," said Beth, with a little sigh, which no one heard but the hearth brush and kettle-holder.

"I shall get a nice box of Faber's drawing pencils; I really need them," said Amy decidedly.

"Mother didn't say anything about our money, and she won't wish us to give up everything. Let's each buy what we want, and have a little fun; I'm sure we work hard enough to earn it," cried Jo, examining the heels of her shoes in a gentlemanly manner.

"I know I do—teaching those tiresome children nearly all day, when I'm longing to enjoy myself at home," began Meg, in the complaining tone again.

"You don't have half such a hard time as I do," said Jo. "How would you like to be shut up for hours with a nervous, fussy old lady, who keeps you trotting, is never satisfied, and worries you till you're ready to fly out the window or cry?"

"It's naughty to fret, but I do think washing dishes and keeping things tidy is the worst work in the world. It makes me cross, and my hands get so stiff, I can't practice well at all." And Beth looked at her rough hands with a sigh that any one could hear that time.

"I don't believe any of you suffer as I do," cried Amy, "for you don't have to go to school with impertinent girls, who plague you if you don't know your lessons, and laugh at your dresses, and label your father if he isn't rich, and insult you when your nose isn't nice."

"If you mean libel, I'd say so, and not talk about labels, as if Papa was a pickle bottle," advised Jo, laughing.

26. Which of the following sentences best describes the theme of this passage?

a. You should always use the biggest words you know.
b. The youngest member of a family should do the most work.
c. Everyone has problems, and it is important to think of others.
d. You should spend your money on yourself because you deserve it.

27. Which choice gives the best summary of the problems presented in this passage?

a. Father is away at war, money is scarce, and the sisters are unhappy with their responsibilities.
b. Mother forbade any presents this Christmas, and the sisters are unhappy with their responsibilities.
c. The sisters do not have as much money to spend as they would like, and Amy is made fun of at school.
d. Beth is tired of cleaning and washing dishes, and Father is away at war.

28. What do you know to be true about Father?

a. He wants the sisters to spend their money on themselves.
b. He misses his wife and children.
c. He wants the sisters to give their money to the army.
d. He is with the army.

29. What do you know to be true about Mother?

a. She misses her husband.
b. She is sorry that the family is poor.
c. She proposed not having presents.
d. She wants the sisters to spend their money on themselves.

30. Who is the only sister who does NOT specify what she wants to buy with her money?

a. Amy
b. Beth
c. Jo
d. Meg

31. What is Amy's primary grievance?

a. Having sisters who laugh at her
b. Having to attend school with impertinent girls
c. Having a mother who told her not to spend money
d. Having difficulty with understanding uncommon words

32. Which of the following statements best describes the relationship between the sisters and Father?

a. The sisters are angry with Father for going away.
b. The sisters know that Mother misses Father.
c. The sisters love and miss Father.
d. The sisters are upset that Father isn't rich.

33. What does the phrase "ought to" mean in the context of this selection?

"We can't do much, but we can make our little sacrifices, and ought to do it gladly. But I am afraid I don't," and Meg shook her head, as she thought regretfully of all the pretty things she wanted.

a. Don't
b. Want to
c. Can't
d. Should

34. What does the phrase "no one heard bu the hearth brush and kettle holder" tell the reader about where Beth is located in the room?

"I planned to spend mine in new music," said Beth, with a little sigh, which no one heard but the hearth brush and kettle-holder.

a. Near the stove
b. By the window
c. In the kitchen
d. Closest to the fireplace

35. Which of the following is the best description of the way Alcott structured the text in order to create an atmosphere of tension?

a. The characters move from complaints about their lives to things they have to look forward to and back again.
b. The characters are at odds with one another, and the resulting friction creates an atmosphere of tension.
c. The characters agree with each other that their lives are miserable and there is nothing to look forward to.
d. The characters are angry with their parents for being poor.

Questions 36-37 refer to the following excerpt from The Love Song of J. Alfred Prufrock by T.S. Eliot:

No! I am not Prince Hamlet, nor was meant to be;
Am an attendant lord, one that will do
To swell a progress, start a scene or two,
Advise the prince; no doubt, an easy tool,
Deferential, glad to be of use,
Politic, cautious, and meticulous;
Full of high sentence, but a bit obtuse;
At times, indeed, almost ridiculous—
Almost, at times, the Fool.
I grow old ... I grow old ...
I shall wear the bottoms of my trousers rolled.
Shall I part my hair behind? Do I dare to eat a peach?
I shall wear white flannel trousers, and walk upon the beach.
I have heard the mermaids singing, each to each.
I do not think that they will sing to me.
I have seen them riding seaward on the waves
Combing the white hair of the waves blown back
When the wind blows the water white and black.
We have lingered in the chambers of the sea

By sea-girls wreathed with seaweed red and brown
Till human voices wake us, and we drown.

36. The first stanza refers to the play *Hamlet, Prince of Denmark* by William Shakespeare. Which of the following best describes Prufrock's description of himself in comparison with the characters in *Hamlet, Prince of Denmark*?

a. Prufrock concludes that he is like Prince Hamlet because they are both majestic and charismatic.
b. Prufrock concludes that he is not like Prince Hamlet, but rather like an obsequious attendant to the prince.
c. Prufrock concludes that he and Hamlet are both fools.
d. Prufrock concludes that he is not like any of the characters in *Hamlet, Prince of Denmark*.

37. The last stanza refers to the song of the Sirens in Homer's *Odyssey*. The song was said to be so alluring that sailors would be driven mad with their desperation to reach the Sirens. With that in mind, identify the best analysis of the following lines:

"I have heard the mermaids singing, each to each.

I do not think that they will sing to me."

a. Prufrock believes that he is just imagining the mermaids' song, so it can't hurt him.
b. Prufrock believes he is strong enough to resist the temptation of the mermaids' song.
c. Prufrock believes that he is not worthy of the attention of the mermaids.
d. Prufrock believes that he will die because of the allure of the mermaids' song.

38. Choose the sentence that most effectively follows the conventions of Standard Written English:

a. Betty MacDonald became famous for her first novel, *The Egg and I*, which chronicles her adventures in chicken farming.
b. *The Egg and I*, a book written by Betty MacDonald, made the book's author famous and chronicled her adventures in chicken farming.
c. Betty MacDonald wrote *The Egg and I*, and became famous chronicling her adventures in chicken farming.
d. *The Egg and I* chronicles the author's adventures in chicken farming, and made Betty MacDonald famous.

39. Choose the sentence that most effectively follows the conventions of Standard Written English:

a. Wilbur and Orville Wright were two brothers, and they tested their prototype airplane on a beach in Kitty Hawk, North Carolina.
b. The two brothers, Wilbur and Orville Wright, tested their prototype airplane on a beach in Kitty Hawk, North Carolina.
c. Testing their prototype airplane on a beach in Kitty Hawk, North Carolina, were the two brothers, Wilbur and Orville Wright.
d. The beach in Kitty Hawk, North Carolina was where the two brothers, Wilbur and Orville Wright, came and tested their prototype airplane.

Directions for questions 40-42: Read the following sentences. Choose the underlined word or phrase that should be changed so that the sentence follows the conventions of Standard Written English. For sentences that are correct as written, choose option D.

40. Our teacher gave Selena and me extra homework after we were caught talking in class.

a. Selena and me
b. homework after
c. were caught
d. No error

41. The movie effected Penelope so profoundly that her life was changed forever.

a. effected Penelope
b. profoundly that
c. changed forever
d. No error

42. The teacher announced that everybody would need to take their own chair to the concert on the front lawn.

a. that everybody
b. their own
c. concert on
d. No error

43. Choose the words that best fill the blanks in the following sentence:
Harper Lee wrote *To Kill a Mockingbird* as an ______ of social ______.

a. argument, dance
b. incident, class
c. exposé, injustice
d. ulterior, inequalities

44. Choose the words that best fill the blanks in the following sentence:
The Statue of Liberty, a ________ to the people of the United States from the people of France, is a ________ of freedom from tyranny.

a. gift, symbol
b. statue, present
c. representing, law
d. decision, ruler

Questions 45-48 refer to the following paragraph:

The students took turns going to the podium. One by one, words were given, pronounced, and spelled. Each word was a test all its own. Students who did not pass the test were returned to the audience. Now there were only two students left. They asked for definitions and origins. They spelled word after word with no mistakes. Just when the tension in the room reached its peak, the word given was too great a trial, and the contestants were reduced again by one.

45. Which of the following would be the best introductory sentence for this paragraph?

a. The lights in the auditorium were too bright.
b. The contestants were dressed up for this important occasion.
c. It was time for the school's annual spelling bee.
d. The students would eat lunch in the auditorium after the spelling bee.

46. Which of the following would be the best sentence to add sensory detail to the paragraph?

a. Several members of the audience twisted their hands in an unconscious expression of anxiety.
b. Trickles of sweat brought on by nerves and the lights ran down the faces of the remaining two contestants.
c. The heat from the lights reached out to the audience, and many were forced to remove their jackets.
d. Students outside the auditorium heard the roar of the audience as they hurried to classes.

47. Which of the following would be the best sentence to add descriptive detail to this paragraph?

a. The last two contestants twisted in their seats, miniature tornadoes of nerves and sweat, ready to face a destruction of their own making.
b. The contestants were nervous.
c. The bright orange of the moderator's jacket stood out in the crowd.
d. The scene outside the window was pastoral.

48. Which of the following would be the best concluding sentence for this paragraph?

a. The shriek of feedback from the sound system startled the contestants.
b. The participants' voices could be heard clearly all over the auditorium as they took turns spelling.
c. The contestants filed up on to the stage to take their positions.
d. The contest was over, and the trophy was finally presented.

Questions 49-54 refer to the following paragraph:

The majority of fish live in a group called a school. The school keeps its members safer from predators than they would be swimming alone. Ants live in large communities called colonies. Each ant in the colony has an assigned job. Ants are strong insects known to be able to lift many times their own weight. Wolves live in family groups called packs that work together to find food and raise their young.

49. Which of the following would be the best introductory sentence for this paragraph?

a. Young wolves are called pups.
b. Ants are dedicated to the survival of their community.
c. Many different species of animals live in cooperative groups.
d. Fish in a school swim closely together.

50. Which of the following sentences is the best fit to add information to this paragraph?

a. Sharks are a type of fish.
b. Ant colonies are organized around a queen.
c. Small fish often become prey for larger fish.
d. Wolves are carnivores that eat deer, elk, and moose.

51. Which of the following sentences does NOT fit the primary premise of the paragraph?

a. Tigers live and hunt alone.
b. Coyotes live in family groups.
c. Bottlenose dolphins form groups called pods.
d. Female alligators create nests on land for their eggs.

52. Which of the following would be the best introductory sentence for a paragraph that follows and connects to this paragraph?

a. Working together allows animal groups to hunt more efficiently.
b. Many animals have coloring and markings that allow them to blend into their surroundings.
c. Monarch butterflies have an average life span of six to eight months.
d. Some animals, such as chipmunks, store food while it is plentiful to be used later when food is scarce.

53. Which of the following sentences is NOT essential to explain the primary premise of the paragraph?

a. The majority of fish live in a group called a school.
b. Ants live in large communities called colonies.
c. Each ant in the colony has an assigned job.
d. Ants are strong insects known to be able to lift many times their own weight.

54. Which of the following would be the best concluding sentence for this paragraph?

a. Living and working together helps many animal species survive.
b. Lions live in cooperative groups called prides, but tigers live alone.
c. Wolves are ready to hunt with the pack when they are six months old.
d. It is important for ants to work together in order to survive.

Answers and Explanations

ELA-Literacy.L.9-10.2a

1. D: "Sonja works very hard" and "she is tired all the time" are both independent clauses (they contain a subject and a verb and express a complete thought). It is appropriate to join two independent clauses with a semicolon. Choice A is a comma splice. Choice B is a run-on sentence. Choice C incorrectly uses a comma to precede the conjunctive adverb "however."

ELA-Literacy.L.9-10.1b

2. A: The highlighted words contain a subject and a verb and express a complete thought (the requirements of an independent clause), but the dependent marker word "although" has been added.

ELA-Literacy.L.9-10.1a

3. A: "Answer" (present tense form of the verb) maintains the parallel structure of the sentence and matches the verb tense of the words "get" and "read." The other answer choices represent the present participle ("answering"), infinitive ("to answer"), and future tense ("will answer").

ELA-Literacy.L.9-10.2c

4. B: The correct spelling of the word is "deleterious."

ELA-Literacy.L.9-10.2b

5. D: It is appropriate to use a colon to introduce a list. It is not appropriate to use a colon following a preposition (choice B), or after the phrases "including" and "for example" as used in choices A and C, which make the use of a colon redundant.

ELA-Literacy.L.9-10.4a

6. C: The context of the sentence and use of the phrase "quickly moving on" indicate that the immigration officer is in a hurry and does not spend a lot of time examining Maria's passport.

ELA-Literacy.L.9-10.4b

7. B: "Representative" acts as a noun and "represent" as a verb. The sentence should read: As a student council representative, Travis endeavored to represent his peers to the best of his ability.

ELA-Literacy.L.9-10.5a

8. C: Personification is an expression in which animals or objects are given human characteristics. In this sentence, the trees are given the human ability to wave a fond farewell.

ELA-Literacy.L.9-10.6

9. B: The word "arbitrary" means random or determined by chance. The sentence should read: The selection of the winning lottery numbers is entirely arbitrary with numbers being drawn at random out of a large ball.

ELA-Literacy.L.9-10.5a

10. A: The context of the sentence and use of the phrase "the surprise was ruined" indicate that Theresa told Margaret about the party.

ELA-Literacy.RI.9-10.3

11. B: The passage discusses Helen Keller's life beginning with her birth and continuing on into her adulthood.

ELA-Literacy.RI.9-10.2

12. A: Although all of the answer choices are true, only choice A focuses on both Helen's journey to overcome her disabilities and Anne Sullivan's involvement.

ELA-Literacy.RI.9-10.6

13. D: The passage does mention that Helen graduated from Radcliffe College (choice A), and the passage does tell about Anne's role as Helen's teacher (choice B), but the passage as a whole does not focus on Helen's time at college or Anne's life outside of her role as teacher. The passage does not mention services available for the deaf and blind (choice C). The passage does tell about Helen Keller's life.

ELA-Literacy.RI.9-10.3

14. C: The second paragraph explains why Anne Sullivan was crucial to Helen's life, and the third paragraph elaborates on how Anne helped Helen succeed.

ELA-Literacy.RI.9-10.6

15. C: The author's use of the phrase "Helen learned at an incredible rate" and the word "remarkable" to describe Helen's life are two examples of the author's admiration.

ELA-Literacy.RI.9-10.1

16. B: The passage states: "Helen herself was easily frustrated and lonely in her dark, silent world." Being unable to see or hear left Helen with no alternatives for communication beyond temper tantrums. It was not until Anne Sullivan became Helen's teacher that Helen learned to communicate her thoughts in a positive way.

ELA-Literacy.RI.9-10.1

17. D: Although all of the answer choices represent major events in Helen's life, the passage specifies that the advent of Anne Sullivan was the turning point in Helen's life when she began to learn to communicate with other people. "All of that began to change in March 1887 when Anne Sullivan came to live with the Kellers and be Helen's teacher. Anne taught Helen to communicate by forming letters with her fingers held in another person's hand."

ELA-Literacy.RI.9-10.1

18. A: The passage does not indicate that Helen's parents were jealous of Anne (choice B), glad to give Anne responsibility for Helen (choice C), or had any preference in their daughter's choice of a college (choice D). The passage does say that Helen's parents loved her and that they brought Anne to their home to be Helen's teacher. This implies that they were frustrated by their own inability to help Helen and were looking for someone who could.

ELA-Literacy.RI.9-10.4

19. A: "This connection engendered an insatiable curiosity within Helen." The context of this sentence indicates that the connection Helen made between words and the objects they represent caused an insatiable curiosity to exist within Helen.

ELA-Literacy.RI.9-10.4

20. C: "This connection engendered an insatiable curiosity within Helen. After that day, Helen learned at an incredible rate with Teacher by her side." The context of these sentences indicates that Helen's curiosity compelled her to keep learning because her curiosity would never be satisfied.

ELA-Literacy.RI.9-10.8

21. B: The passage does not say that studying a foreign language will help students find jobs after high school (choice A) or gain an understanding of other cultures (choice C). The passage does say that studying a foreign language is important for college acceptance (choice D), but this point alone is not the main idea of the passage.

ELA-Literacy.W.9-10.9b

22. C: The passage does not claim that studying a foreign language is essential to high school graduation (choice A). Choices B and D represent claims made in the passage, but do not include all of the claims made.

ELA-Literacy.SL.9-10.3

23. D: Although students may find knowledge of a foreign language helpful in obtaining a job, it is an obvious exaggeration to claim that students who did not study a foreign language would be unemployable.

ELA-Literacy.W.9-10.8

24. D: Choices A and C represent options that would provide information regarding the opinions of students and parents, but not actual evidence regarding the influence of studying a foreign language on future success. Choice B specifies a second language taught at home, whereas the passage focuses specifically on a foreign language taught in high school.

ELA-Literacy.W.9-10.1e

25. B: Choices A, C, and D do not offer a complete summary of the claims made in this passage.

ELA-Literacy.RL.9-10.2

26. C: The selection does not portray the themes offered in choices A, B, and D.

ELA-Literacy.RL.9-10.2

27. A: Choice B is incorrect because Mother did not forbid any presents. Choices C and D give some of the problems presented in the selection, but do not offer a complete summary.

ELA-Literacy.RL.9-10.1

28. D: The passage states: "'We haven't got Father, and shall not have him for a long time.' She didn't say 'perhaps never,' but each silently added it, thinking of Father far away, where the fighting was." The other choices may be true of Father, but they are not specified in this selection.

ELA-Literacy.RL.9-10.1

29. C: Although choices A and B may be true, they are not specified in this selection. Jo believes choice D to be true, but whether or not she is right is not stated: "'Mother didn't say anything about our money, and she won't wish us to give up everything. Let's each buy what we want, and have a little fun; I'm sure we work hard enough to earn it,' cried Jo."

ELA-Literacy.RL.9-10.1

30. D: The other sisters all specify what they want to buy. Choice A: "'I shall get a nice box of Faber's drawing pencils; I really need them,' said Amy decidedly." Choice B: "'I planned to spend mine in new music,' said Beth." Choice C: "'I do want to buy Undine and Sintran for myself. I've wanted it so long,' said Jo."

ELA-Literacy.RL.9-10.1

31. B: "'I don't believe any of you suffer as I do,' cried Amy, 'for you don't have to go to school with impertinent girls, who plague you if you don't know your lessons, and laugh at your dresses, and label your father if he isn't rich, and insult you when your nose isn't nice.'"

ELA-Literacy.RL.9-10.3

32. C: The passage states: "'We've got Father and Mother, and each other,' said Beth contentedly from her corner. The four young faces on which the firelight shone brightened at the cheerful words, but darkened again as Jo said sadly, 'We haven't got Father, and shall not have him for a long time.' She didn't say 'perhaps never,' but each silently added it, thinking of Father far away, where the fighting was." The sisters are not angry (choice A) or upset (choice D) with Father. The sisters may know that their mother misses their father (choice B), but it is not specified in the passage.

ELA-Literacy.RL.9-10.4

33. D: Meg says that the sisters should be glad to make sacrifices for the army.

ELA-Literacy.RL.9-10.4

34. D: The presence of a hearth brush and kettle-holder indicate a fireplace, and the fact that the fireplace "hears" Beth's sigh when no one else does indicates that Beth is closest to it.

ELA-Literacy.RL.9-10.5

35. A: The sisters start out complaining: "'Christmas won't be Christmas without any presents,' grumbled Jo, lying on the rug. 'It's so dreadful to be poor!' sighed Meg." They move to planning what to buy with their dollar: "Mother didn't say anything about our money, and she won't wish us to give up everything. Let's each buy what we want, and have a little fun." Finally, The sisters are back to lamenting the trials of their situations: "'I don't believe any of you suffer as I do,' cried Amy, 'for you don't have to go to school with impertinent girls.'"

ELA-Literacy.RL.9-10.9

36. B: Prufrock says: "No! I am not Prince Hamlet, nor was meant to be; Am an attendant lord... Deferential, glad to be of use, Politic, cautious, and meticulous."

ELA-Literacy.W.9-10.9a

37. C: Prufrock says: "I grow old ... I grow old ... I shall wear the bottoms of my trousers rolled." He believes that he is too old and unworthy for the mermaids to direct their song toward him.

ELA-Literacy.W.9-10.4

38. A: This sentence best conveys the information without using too many words or having an awkward construction (choices B, C, and D).

ELA-Literacy.W.9-10.4

39. B: This sentence best conveys the information without using too many words (choice D) or having an awkward construction (choices A and B).

ELA-Literacy.W.9-10.5

40. D: The sentence is correct as written.

ELA-Literacy.W.9-10.5

41. A: The sentence should read: The movie affected Penelope so profoundly that her life was changed forever.

ELA-Literacy.W.9-10.5

42. B: The sentence should read: The teacher announced that everybody would need to take his or her own chair to the concert on the front lawn.

ELA-Literacy.W.9-10.4

43. C: The sentence should read: Harper Lee wrote *To Kill a Mockingbird* as an exposé of social injustice.

ELA-Literacy.W.9-10.4

44. A: The sentence should read: The Statue of Liberty, a gift to the people of the United States from the people of France, is a symbol of freedom from tyranny.

ELA-Literacy.W.9-10.3a

45. C: Choices A and B are detail sentences. Choice D references an event outside the time frame included in the rest of the paragraph.

ELA-Literacy.W.9-10.3d

46. B: This is the only choice that expands on the feelings of the spelling bee contestants. The focus of the paragraph is on the contestants, not the audience (choices A and C) nor the students who are not participating in the spelling bee (choice D).

ELA-Literacy.W.9-10.3b

47. A: This is the only choice that focuses on the contestants and uses descriptive language to give the reader a picture of the scene. Choice B tells how the contestants felt, but does not use descriptive language. Choices C and D are descriptive sentences, but do not refer to the contestants, who are the main focus of the paragraph.

ELA-Literacy.W.9-10.3e

48. D: This is the only sentence of the given choices that sums up the events of the paragraph. Choices A and B focus on the events of the paragraph, but do not bring them to a resolution. Choice C focuses on a time period before the events of the paragraph.

ELA-Literacy.W.9-10.2a

49. C: The other choices are detail sentences and do not express the main idea of the paragraph.

ELA-Literacy.W.9-10.2d

50. B: This is the only sentence that focuses on the organization of an animal group.

ELA-Literacy.W.9-10.2e

51. D: All of the other choices provide information about whether or not animals live in cooperative groups.

ELA-Literacy.W.9-10.10

52. A: This is the only sentence that connects to the first paragraph by continuing to expound upon the premise of animals living in cooperative groups.

ELA-Literacy.W.9-10.2b

53. D: Of the choices given, this is the only sentence that does not add to the premise that many species of animals live in cooperative groups.

ELA-Literacy.W.9-10.2f

54. A: This is the only choice that sums up the tone and purpose of the paragraph. Choices C and D are detail sentences, and choice B introduces two animals not mentioned in the paragraph.

How to Overcome Test Anxiety

Just the thought of taking a test is enough to make most people a little nervous. A test is an important event that can have a long-term impact on your future, so it's important to take it seriously and it's natural to feel anxious about performing well. But just because anxiety is normal, that doesn't mean that it's helpful in test taking, or that you should simply accept it as part of your life. Anxiety can have a variety of effects. These effects can be mild, like making you feel slightly nervous, or severe, like blocking your ability to focus or remember even a simple detail.

If you experience test anxiety—whether severe or mild—it's important to know how to beat it. To discover this, first you need to understand what causes test anxiety.

Causes of Test Anxiety

While we often think of anxiety as an uncontrollable emotional state, it can actually be caused by simple, practical things. One of the most common causes of test anxiety is that a person does not feel adequately prepared for their test. This feeling can be the result of many different issues such as poor study habits or lack of organization, but the most common culprit is time management. Starting to study too late, failing to organize your study time to cover all of the material, or being distracted while you study will mean that you're not well prepared for the test. This may lead to cramming the night before, which will cause you to be physically and mentally exhausted for the test. Poor time management also contributes to feelings of stress, fear, and hopelessness as you realize you are not well prepared but don't know what to do about it.

Other times, test anxiety is not related to your preparation for the test but comes from unresolved fear. This may be a past failure on a test, or poor performance on tests in general. It may come from comparing yourself to others who seem to be performing better or from the stress of living up to expectations. Anxiety may be driven by fears of the future—how failure on this test would affect your educational and career goals. These fears are often completely irrational, but they can still negatively impact your test performance.

Elements of Test Anxiety

As mentioned earlier, test anxiety is considered to be an emotional state, but it has physical and mental components as well. Sometimes you may not even realize that you are suffering from test anxiety until you notice the physical symptoms. These can include trembling hands, rapid heartbeat, sweating, nausea, and tense muscles. Extreme anxiety may lead to fainting or vomiting. Obviously, any of these symptoms can have a negative impact on testing. It is important to recognize them as soon as they begin to occur so that you can address the problem before it damages your performance.

The mental components of test anxiety include trouble focusing and inability to remember learned information. During a test, your mind is on high alert, which can help you recall information and stay focused for an extended period of time. However, anxiety interferes with your mind's natural processes, causing you to blank out, even on the questions you know well. The strain of testing during anxiety makes it difficult to stay focused, especially on a test that may take several hours. Extreme anxiety can take a huge mental toll, making it difficult not only to recall test information but even to understand the test questions or pull your thoughts together.

Effects of Test Anxiety

Test anxiety is like a disease—if left untreated, it will get progressively worse. Anxiety leads to poor performance, and this reinforces the feelings of fear and failure, which in turn lead to poor performances on subsequent tests. It can grow from a mild nervousness to a crippling condition. If allowed to progress, test anxiety can have a big impact on your schooling, and consequently on your future.

Test anxiety can spread to other parts of your life. Anxiety on tests can become anxiety in any stressful situation, and blanking on a test can turn into panicking in a job situation. But fortunately, you don't have to let anxiety rule your testing and determine your grades. There are a number of relatively simple steps you can take to move past anxiety and function normally on a test and in the rest of life.

Physical Steps for Beating Test Anxiety

While test anxiety is a serious problem, the good news is that it can be overcome. It doesn't have to control your ability to think and remember information. While it may take time, you can begin taking steps today to beat anxiety.

Just as your first hint that you may be struggling with anxiety comes from the physical symptoms, the first step to treating it is also physical. Rest is crucial for having a clear, strong mind. If you are tired, it is much easier to give in to anxiety. But if you establish good sleep habits, your body and mind will be ready to perform optimally, without the strain of exhaustion. Additionally, sleeping well helps you to retain information better, so you're more likely to recall the answers when you see the test questions.

Getting good sleep means more than going to bed on time. It's important to allow your brain time to relax. Take study breaks from time to time so it doesn't get overworked, and don't study right before bed. Take time to rest your mind before trying to rest your body, or you may find it difficult to fall asleep.

Along with sleep, other aspects of physical health are important in preparing for a test. Good nutrition is vital for good brain function. Sugary foods and drinks may give a burst of energy but this burst is followed by a crash, both physically and emotionally. Instead, fuel your body with protein and vitamin-rich foods.

Also, drink plenty of water. Dehydration can lead to headaches and exhaustion, especially if your brain is already under stress from the rigors of the test. Particularly if your test is a long one, drink water during the breaks. And if possible, take an energy-boosting snack to eat between sections.

Along with sleep and diet, a third important part of physical health is exercise. Maintaining a steady workout schedule is helpful, but even taking 5-minute study breaks to walk can help get your blood pumping faster and clear your head. Exercise also releases endorphins, which contribute to a positive feeling and can help combat test anxiety.

When you nurture your physical health, you are also contributing to your mental health. If your body is healthy, your mind is much more likely to be healthy as well. So take time to rest, nourish your body with healthy food and water, and get moving as much as possible. Taking these physical steps will make you stronger and more able to take the mental steps necessary to overcome test anxiety.

Mental Steps for Beating Test Anxiety

Working on the mental side of test anxiety can be more challenging, but as with the physical side, there are clear steps you can take to overcome it. As mentioned earlier, test anxiety often stems from lack of preparation, so the obvious solution is to prepare for the test. Effective studying may be the most important weapon you have for beating test anxiety, but you can and should employ several other mental tools to combat fear.

First, boost your confidence by reminding yourself of past success—tests or projects that you aced. If you're putting as much effort into preparing for this test as you did for those, there's no reason you should expect to fail here. Work hard to prepare; then trust your preparation.

Second, surround yourself with encouraging people. It can be helpful to find a study group, but be sure that the people you're around will encourage a positive attitude. If you spend time with others who are anxious or cynical, this will only contribute to your own anxiety. Look for others who are motivated to study hard from a desire to succeed, not from a fear of failure.

Third, reward yourself. A test is physically and mentally tiring, even without anxiety, and it can be helpful to have something to look forward to. Plan an activity following the test, regardless of the outcome, such as going to a movie or getting ice cream.

When you are taking the test, if you find yourself beginning to feel anxious, remind yourself that you know the material. Visualize successfully completing the test. Then take a few deep, relaxing breaths and return to it. Work through the questions carefully but with confidence, knowing that you are capable of succeeding.

Developing a healthy mental approach to test taking will also aid in other areas of life. Test anxiety affects more than just the actual test—it can be damaging to your mental health and even contribute to depression. It's important to beat test anxiety before it becomes a problem for more than testing.

Study Strategy

Being prepared for the test is necessary to combat anxiety, but what does being prepared look like? You may study for hours on end and still not feel prepared. What you need is a strategy for test prep. The next few pages outline our recommended steps to help you plan out and conquer the challenge of preparation.

Step 1: Scope Out the Test

Learn everything you can about the format (multiple choice, essay, etc.) and what will be on the test. Gather any study materials, course outlines, or sample exams that may be available. Not only will this help you to prepare, but knowing what to expect can help to alleviate test anxiety.

Step 2: Map Out the Material

Look through the textbook or study guide and make note of how many chapters or sections it has. Then divide these over the time you have. For example, if a book has 15 chapters and you have five days to study, you need to cover three chapters each day. Even better, if you have the time, leave an extra day at the end for overall review after you have gone through the material in depth.

If time is limited, you may need to prioritize the material. Look through it and make note of which sections you think you already have a good grasp on, and which need review. While you are studying, skim quickly through the familiar sections and take more time on the challenging parts.

Write out your plan so you don't get lost as you go. Having a written plan also helps you feel more in control of the study, so anxiety is less likely to arise from feeling overwhelmed at the amount to cover.

Step 3: Gather Your Tools

Decide what study method works best for you. Do you prefer to highlight in the book as you study and then go back over the highlighted portions? Or do you type out notes of the important information? Or is it helpful to make flashcards that you can carry with you? Assemble the pens, index cards, highlighters, post-it notes, and any other materials you may need so you won't be distracted by getting up to find things while you study.

If you're having a hard time retaining the information or organizing your notes, experiment with different methods. For example, try color-coding by subject with colored pens, highlighters, or post-it notes. If you learn better by hearing, try recording yourself reading your notes so you can listen while in the car, working out, or simply sitting at your desk. Ask a friend to quiz you from your flashcards, or try teaching someone the material to solidify it in your mind.

Step 4: Create Your Environment

It's important to avoid distractions while you study. This includes both the obvious distractions like visitors and the subtle distractions like an uncomfortable chair (or a too-comfortable couch that makes you want to fall asleep). Set up the best study environment possible: good lighting and a comfortable work area. If background music helps you focus, you may want to turn it on, but otherwise keep the room quiet. If you are using a computer to take notes, be sure you don't have any other windows open, especially applications like social media, games, or anything else that could distract you. Silence your phone and turn off notifications. Be sure to keep water close by so you stay hydrated while you study (but avoid unhealthy drinks and snacks).

Also, take into account the best time of day to study. Are you freshest first thing in the morning? Try to set aside some time then to work through the material. Is your mind clearer in the afternoon or evening? Schedule your study session then. Another method is to study at the same time of day that you will take the test, so that your brain gets used to working on the material at that time and will be ready to focus at test time.

Step 5: Study!

Once you have done all the study preparation, it's time to settle into the actual studying. Sit down, take a few moments to settle your mind so you can focus, and begin to follow your study plan. Don't give in to distractions or let yourself procrastinate. This is your time to prepare so you'll be ready to fearlessly approach the test. Make the most of the time and stay focused.

Of course, you don't want to burn out. If you study too long you may find that you're not retaining the information very well. Take regular study breaks. For example, taking five minutes out of every hour to walk briskly, breathing deeply and swinging your arms, can help your mind stay fresh.

As you get to the end of each chapter or section, it's a good idea to do a quick review. Remind yourself of what you learned and work on any difficult parts. When you feel that you've mastered the material, move on to the next part. At the end of your study session, briefly skim through your notes again.

But while review is helpful, cramming last minute is NOT. If at all possible, work ahead so that you won't need to fit all your study into the last day. Cramming overloads your brain with more information than it can process and retain, and your tired mind may struggle to recall even previously learned information when it is overwhelmed with last-minute study. Also, the urgent nature of cramming and the stress placed on your brain contribute to anxiety. You'll be more likely to go to the test feeling unprepared and having trouble thinking clearly.

So don't cram, and don't stay up late before the test, even just to review your notes at a leisurely pace. Your brain needs rest more than it needs to go over the information again. In fact, plan to finish your studies by noon or early afternoon the day before the test. Give your brain the rest of the day to relax or focus on other things, and get a good night's sleep. Then you will be fresh for the test and better able to recall what you've studied.

Step 6: Take a Practice Test

Many courses offer sample tests, either online or in the study materials. This is an excellent resource to check whether you have mastered the material, as well as to prepare for the test format and environment.

Check the test format ahead of time: the number of questions, the type (multiple choice, free response, etc.), and the time limit. Then create a plan for working through them. For example, if you have 30 minutes to take a 60-question test, your limit is 30 seconds per question. Spend less time on the questions you know well so that you can take more time on the difficult ones.

If you have time to take several practice tests, take the first one open book, with no time limit. Work through the questions at your own pace and make sure you fully understand them. Gradually work up to taking a test under test conditions: sit at a desk with all study materials put away and set a timer. Pace yourself to make sure you finish the test with time to spare and go back to check your answers if you have time.

After each test, check your answers. On the questions you missed, be sure you understand why you missed them. Did you misread the question (tests can use tricky wording)? Did you forget the information? Or was it something you hadn't learned? Go back and study any shaky areas that the practice tests reveal.

Taking these tests not only helps with your grade, but also aids in combating test anxiety. If you're already used to the test conditions, you're less likely to worry about it, and working through tests until you're scoring well gives you a confidence boost. Go through the practice tests until you feel comfortable, and then you can go into the test knowing that you're ready for it.

Test Tips

On test day, you should be confident, knowing that you've prepared well and are ready to answer the questions. But aside from preparation, there are several test day strategies you can employ to maximize your performance.

First, as stated before, get a good night's sleep the night before the test (and for several nights before that, if possible). Go into the test with a fresh, alert mind rather than staying up late to study.

Try not to change too much about your normal routine on the day of the test. It's important to eat a nutritious breakfast, but if you normally don't eat breakfast at all, consider eating just a protein bar. If you're a coffee drinker, go ahead and have your normal coffee. Just make sure you time it so that the caffeine doesn't wear off right in the middle of your test. Avoid sugary beverages, and drink enough water to stay hydrated but not so much that you need a restroom break 10 minutes into the test. If your test isn't first thing in the morning, consider going for a walk or doing a light workout before the test to get your blood flowing.

Allow yourself enough time to get ready, and leave for the test with plenty of time to spare so you won't have the anxiety of scrambling to arrive in time. Another reason to be early is to select a good seat. It's helpful to sit away from doors and windows, which can be distracting. Find a good seat, get out your supplies, and settle your mind before the test begins.

When the test begins, start by going over the instructions carefully, even if you already know what to expect. Make sure you avoid any careless mistakes by following the directions.

Then begin working through the questions, pacing yourself as you've practiced. If you're not sure on an answer, don't spend too much time on it, and don't let it shake your confidence. Either skip it and come back later, or eliminate as many wrong answers as possible and guess among the remaining ones. Don't dwell on these questions as you continue—put them out of your mind and focus on what lies ahead.

Be sure to read all of the answer choices, even if you're sure the first one is the right answer. Sometimes you'll find a better one if you keep reading. But don't second-guess yourself if you do immediately know the answer. Your gut instinct is usually right. Don't let test anxiety rob you of the information you know.

If you have time at the end of the test (and if the test format allows), go back and review your answers. Be cautious about changing any, since your first instinct tends to be correct, but make sure you didn't misread any of the questions or accidentally mark the wrong answer choice. Look over any you skipped and make an educated guess.

At the end, leave the test feeling confident. You've done your best, so don't waste time worrying about your performance or wishing you could change anything. Instead, celebrate the successful completion of this test. And finally, use this test to learn how to deal with anxiety even better next time.

Review Video: Test Anxiety
Visit mometrix.com/academy and enter code: 100340

Important Qualification

Not all anxiety is created equal. If your test anxiety is causing major issues in your life beyond the classroom or testing center, or if you are experiencing troubling physical symptoms related to your anxiety, it may be a sign of a serious physiological or psychological condition. If this sounds like your situation, we strongly encourage you to seek professional help.

Thank You

We at Mometrix would like to extend our heartfelt thanks to you, our friend and patron, for allowing us to play a part in your journey. It is a privilege to serve people from all walks of life who are unified in their commitment to building the best future they can for themselves.

The preparation you devote to these important testing milestones may be the most valuable educational opportunity you have for making a real difference in your life. We encourage you to put your heart into it—that feeling of succeeding, overcoming, and yes, conquering will be well worth the hours you've invested.

We want to hear your story, your struggles and your successes, and if you see any opportunities for us to improve our materials so we can help others even more effectively in the future, please share that with us as well. **The team at Mometrix would be absolutely thrilled to hear from you!** So please, send us an email (support@mometrix.com) and let's stay in touch.

If you'd like some additional help, check out these other resources we offer for your exam:
http://MometrixFlashcards.com/CCSS

Online Resources

Due to our efforts to try to keep this book to a manageable length, we've created a link that will give you access to all of your online resources:

mometrix.com/resources719/ccg9ela

It's Your Moment, Let's Celebrate It!

Share your story @mometrixtestpreparation